Prison to Prosperity
with purpose

A True Story of Redemption

MARSHA MIXON

Prison to Prosperity
with Purpose

A True Story of Redemption

Copyright ©2020 Marsha Mixon

ISBN 979-8-6347221-9-1

All rights reserved. No portion of this publication may be reproduced, stored in a retrieval system, or transmitted in any form or by any means – electronic, mechanical, photocopy, recording, scanning, or other – except for brief quotations, without the prior written permission of the publisher.

Unless otherwise noted, all Scripture quotations are taken from the
New American Standard Bible® (NASB),
Copyright © 1960, 1962, 1963, 1968, 1971, 1972, 1973,
1975, 1977, 1995 by The Lockman Foundation
Used by permission. www.Lockman.org

Printed in the United States of America

Dedication

This book is dedicated to my loving family and my dear friends. Not only did they support me while I was writing this book, but more importantly, they were there for me throughout my long and often painful journey back to the Lord. Although in a different way, they also experienced my journey deep in their very souls.

Words cannot express the sincere sorrow and deep regret I have for the hurt I caused the ones I love the most. Apologies don't seem to be enough for what I put them through during those dark years.

And yet, I know that we can all rejoice and praise the Lord for the forgiveness, redemption, deliverance and restoration that are found in Jesus Christ alone. We can finally celebrate the healing and hope that flows from our relationship with Him.

My mom and dad never stopped loving me unconditionally, and they never stopped praying for me faithfully. No matter how discouraged and desperate I was, they never gave up hope—and they never gave up on me. Today, my blessed and victorious life is a testimony to the fact that the Lord hears and answers the prayers of His children.

My deepest desire for this book is that it would be encourage my parents here on the earth, and that it would be pleasing to my heavenly Father above. Without Him, I can do nothing.

All praise, honor and glory belong to Him alone. Amen.

Contents

Acknowledgments 7

Introduction 9

1 Growing Up: The "Normal" Years 13

2 Sister Christian: Or So I Thought 25

3 Malenka Likes to Drinka: The Plot Thickens 43

4 Redeemed & Restored: All My Hope Is in Jesus 71

5 Path to Prison: Faithful while Fearful 77

6 Restoration & the Road to Prosperity: Life, Take-Two Begins 99

7 Living on Purpose: Finding Your Purpose & Passion 117

A Letter from My Pastor 125

Connecting with Marsha to Speak 129

Acknowledgements
My Heart Is Full of Gratitude

The first acknowledgement that is most fitting for this book is for my Lord and Savior, Jesus Christ. Without Him, I could not have accomplished any of this in my life. He is the reason for it all and it is to give Him glory. Nothing you read is because of me, but because of Him.

Jesus delivered me from a tragic life that was filled with torture and misery. He sent every single person and experience into my life to bring me to this place.

He already knew my purpose and the plans He had to prosper me, not to harm me. He was waiting all along for me to step into my callings and gifts so that His light would shine through me to show the beauty of His grace, love, hope and forgiveness. I am beyond blessed to be saved by Grace.

Next, I want to share my gratitude to my amazing team that God sent help me gather resources and brainstorm ideas.

Lynn Rentz Adcox	Kathy Guerry
Karen Bunch Franklin	Jennifer Villines
Jessica Davis	Lyndee Kinard

And finally, I want to give a very special acknowledgement to my son, *Christopher Campbell*.

Son, you are my side-kick and my right arm! Thank you for all of your love, support, encouragement, nagging, prodding, diligence, hard work, tolerance, patience and dedication!

Truly, without you, none of this could ever have been accomplished. We make an amazing team and I am so blessed to see you thrive and succeed. More than that, I am blessed to see your commitment to Christ. You are a true man of God and your spirit always shines so bright in your service. Mom loves and appreciates you more than you will ever know.

Love, Mom

Introduction

Throughout my whole life, I've felt as if I should write a book. The problem is, I never had an ending for it. I had multiple beginnings, dramatic plot twists and tragedies, but there was no happy ending or storyline that would provide any value to readers.

I was a pretty boring kid. I grew up in a two-parent home with just one sibling. I grew up in a small town and was raised in a stable Christian home. Then, at the age of 17, things began to change. I got my first boyfriend, a man I would marry just a month after graduation. This would be the start of my lifelong pattern of engaging in unhealthy relationships.

While that may seem like a decent book in itself, there was much more to my story. Although I had four failed marriages, the deeper issues would show that these were simply a byproduct of what was going on spiritually, mentally, emotionally and physically in my life.

I had zero self-esteem, and lacked the vision, ambition and ability to position myself in a place where I felt I was able to succeed. I can literally sum it all up in one word—obesity. I was always the chubby kid. The one with the thick thighs. Back then, it was not "in" to have extra junk in the trunk.

As the years passed, I jumped from one relationship to another, each relationship marred by my cheating, drug and alcohol use, promiscuity, mental and physical abuse and financial irresponsibility. I found myself repeatedly holding what one would consider a full house. I had experienced it all. Everything that could go wrong in a marriage, did.

My empty, unhappy life began to build up over the years and ultimately led me to a lifestyle filled with wild partying, drug abuse, alcoholism, attempted suicide and living a life that was a complete abomination to my faith, all the while attempting to raise my four children and provide for them, mostly on my own.

The breaking point came when I was facing prison time. I had never been in trouble before, at least not of this magnitude, and it was time to pay the piper. I lost everything. While incarcerated for 192 days, I was evicted from my home. After much soul searching, I discovered this truth—I was able to persevere each and every moment throughout my sentence and remain devout after my release because of one thing—my faith in God, and my assurance that He had a specific plan for *me*. My faith opened my eyes and helped me see that I was now in a position to begin sharing my story of hope so I can inspire others who have experienced similar pain.

I believe this book will inspire you. Please allow me to take you through this journey with me—a journey that I feared would never end well. I believe it must be shared. It is never too late. As long as you have breath in your body, there is hope.

This book is written not to impress you, but to impress upon you

INTRODUCTION

that if God will do it for me, He will do it for you. He will do it for your loved one. He will show up in the darkness and His grace, love and salvation will overcome it all.

It is my prayer that this book inspires you to search within yourself and ask the questions, "What is my purpose? What am I passionate about? How can God use me? What did He create me to be in this world?"

All of these answers are already there. You just have to be willing to allow God to show you. Join me as I share my story of how I went from *Prison to Prosperity*.

CHAPTER 1

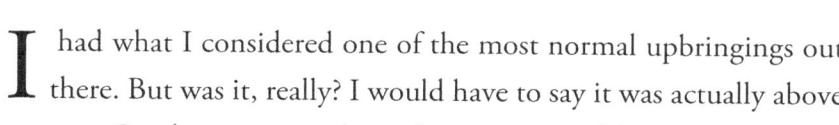

The "Normal" Years

I had what I considered one of the most normal upbringings out there. But was it, really? I would have to say it was actually above average. Our house was a place where everyone felt "at home" when they visited. It was full of love. No one ever said it felt cold or distant. We welcomed and loved on everyone.

We always had Jeep rides, horses, gardens, bunnies, puppies, chickens and even a cow. My parents made everything an adventure. We fished, hunted, played and just always had a great time together. Honestly, I could not have asked for a better upbringing. I was blessed to have a two-parent home full of love. They were strict, but not too strict. They did not argue and they respected one another. My parents were, in all honesty, the perfect example. Our family has been filled with love, even when we disagreed; and boy, did we ever disagree.

On the other hand, we didn't really have a large group of friends with whom we regularly interacted on a deep level, even though we knew a lot of people. Why? I don't know. But I suspect, for me anyway, it was my lack of self-confidence. Maybe it was a lack of trust due to my own way of thinking. These are questions to which I still do not have answers. And, if I am realistic about it, I still live in a very small world. I don't have cliques or a revolving door of friends I share a ton of time with on a daily basis.

I believe the mindset I cultivated created a feeling of unworthiness. That feeling still wants to rear its ugly face and tell me I don't belong. But why did I believe I didn't belong in the first place? Because I didn't feel like I ever fit in. I was the circle standing in front of a square. I saw myself as seriously overweight. Looking back, I'm in shock because I was not even that big. But I felt inferior. I felt like I stuck out like a sore thumb.

I recall shopping at our local department store. It was pricey for my parents, no doubt. But because I was the heavy kid, that is where we ended up and they sacrificed the extra money in an attempt to help me fit in. At school, my clothes were always different. But I also had to shop in the plus sizes, so this made me stand out because they were not like the in-style skinny girl clothes everyone else had. *That* was the *last thing* I wanted to do.

I always tried to hide. Behind people, clothes, family and home. I felt safe at home. I belonged there. I was accepted there. I was loved there. Nowhere else did I feel that way.

In our home, we loved to celebrate; and we celebrated with food.

GROWING UP: The "Normal" Years

We all were amazing cooks and could whip up more deliciousness than you can imagine in no time flat. It was a craft. A craft we had quite honestly, *mastered*. Boy, oh boy, did the scales reflect that fact. I am sure you have heard the phrase, never trust a skinny cook, right? Well, we were 100% trustworthy, without a doubt.

When you're overweight, you know it. You don't need anyone telling you. So, we tried to help each other. I recall "dieting" from a very young age. I just never could achieve the success I wanted. My comfort food was whisked away and replaced with things like sugar loaded grapefruit, dry toast, salad and broccoli. Oh, and green beans and baked chicken, let's not leave those out. What 11-year-old doesn't dig a salad, right? I didn't, that's for sure.

This resulted in shameful behaviors. I recall one weight loss support group specifically, T.O.P.S. It stood for "Take Off Pounds Sensibly." We would tout the phrase as a group: "Even though I overeat in private, my excess baggage is there for all the world to see." If you gained weight that week, as I recall, there was some sort of pig trophy you had the pleasure of taking home to stare you in the eye and guilt you into action. I can still see this evil little piggy grinning at me with disdain over my cheating.

I'm certain that some well-intentioned person created that statement and that little piggy in an effort to help the masses "Take Off Pounds Sensibly." After all, we met weekly to support one another. We celebrated our victories. We counted our calories. Guess what else we did? As soon as that meeting was over, we all landed our broad behinds in the local Shoney's to load up on more carbs, treats, gravies and goodies to seek comfort once again. It was a vicious cycle. It was a very vicious and very unproductive cycle.

As you can imagine, my family felt the unintentional negative effects of this mantra and weekly reinforcement. This ultimately led to another failure. The battle of the weight continued on and on for decades. But the effects of that statement stuck strongly and fueled those feelings of failure and inferiority.

As I progressed through my academic years, I continued with this timid, low self-esteem mindset. I was not active in academic groups. I didn't participate in activities like our French class trip to Quebec. I didn't go on our Senior Cruise. I barely went to prom. I just didn't feel good enough and I always felt like I didn't belong.

I met my first husband when I was 17 years old, and I thought I was in love. He was over the moon about me, or so I thought, and we ultimately married. However, prior to that marriage, he had cheated on me with his child's mother and another child was conceived from that infidelity.

Did I marry him anyway? You betcha. I was out to prove that I was *better*. Boy was I lost in my thinking. I should have quickly just ended it all and moved on, confident that I was a catch for the right one. I should have gone on to college and lived my life. But I chose not to do any of this. I chose to jump into a marriage that was bound to fail from the start.

GROWING UP: The "Normal" Years

Our lives pretty much centered around drinking and smoking pot. Sadly, my memories of this entire part of my life are extremely dim. It's like a blank. Maybe it's a protection mechanism created in my mind. But when I try to draw on memories of that time period—there just aren't any. Not even of the wedding day. I can't even tell you who was there on a day that should have been etched in my memory for life.

College? Let's just touch on that one for a bit. In my 11th grade year, I felt so unworthy, I began to dabble in marijuana and booze. Although I had been a high achiever academically, I now had lost interest in that area. I was accepted by a group of misfits, and they didn't seem to care that I was overweight. Therefore, I quickly pursued that lifestyle.

I had the guidance counselor tell me that I wasn't "college material." Let's call her "Mrs. Flower." She crushed me in that single moment of time, and she'll never truly know how much that one statement profoundly affected every day of my life going forward. I questioned even bothering to graduate from high school if I wasn't college material? I mean, what was the point?

To this day, I understand this is a common practice among guidance counselors. They are literally judge and jury as to whether a student is fit for college—and when they believe you're not a fit, they tell you. Why? I have absolutely no idea. Who knows? Maybe my putting it out there in writing will create the need for change in this area. I think I'm doing pretty well, in spite of it all.

If the concept of college had been portrayed as something I could have achieved, then I think I would have pursued it. My parents couldn't afford it, and we really had no idea about how we would pay for it otherwise. As a result, I slipped into a sub-standard life. I'm 100% certain my life has shown that believing in an individual and sharing that belief can create massive change. This is exactly why I am so passionate about belief. You never know what *your* belief in another person can accomplish.

I would like to challenge you right now to think of someone whom you think may need some belief in themselves. Pour into them positive words, show them encouragement, and even share this book with them to let them know how much you believe in them. Make a note below to them as to why you believe in them and share this with them. You may create the change in their life that they are longing to experience.

_____

_____

_____

_____

Okay, I know that was random, but I felt inspired by the Lord to call you to action. Sometimes, that's all it takes.

Now, back to that guidance counselor: When someone with a

GROWING UP: The "Normal" Years

degree and whose profession is guiding students to success tells you that you're no good, it does something to you. When she told me I wasn't college material, it felt like a switch was flipped. Every inferior thought I ever had was completely validated in that moment in time. I recall the dark, cold feeling of that office. Her perfect little life portrayed on her desk in photos of her family and *my* feeling like I would never achieve anything. So, I just gave up. I decided high school wasn't for me. My mindset was to just quit and be a drop out. Why not? Even a professional told me it was no use trying for more.

Somehow, my mother talked me into a conference with the District Superintendent of the schools for our county. I don't recall what he said specifically. I can't even remember what he looked like. But whatever he said made an impression. He made a difference. I went back to school determined to finish strong. I finished my senior year with an A-B average and was quite proud of myself.

Sadly, I don't recall those words of affirmation he spoke to me. I don't recall a quote. I don't recall the specifics. But I do remember how he made me *feel*. It was in direct contrast to how Mrs. Flower made me feel—no doubt. Yet, I remembered her words—verbatim.

What does that say about my psychological state and how I viewed myself? I was strong enough to believe as much as he had poured into me—to complete high school. But I never did complete a college degree. Thirty-two years later, at 49 years old, I can say with certainty that the way she made me *feel* has always stuck with me. But every time I recount that story, I have the amazing story of how that superintendent spoke with me.

I suppose I'll need to find it somewhere in my heart to forgive her, even be thankful for her. Of course, without that happening, I would not be the person I'm so proud of today. I wouldn't have this story to tell. I wouldn't be able to encourage the masses. I wouldn't have the level of passion that I do. So, Mrs. Flower, I want to tell you that I forgive you, wherever you might be in this world.

Seldom do we take time out to build people up. As a result, we all walk around broken and defeated. Then there are those situations when we are the ones who pour into others because it makes us feel better about ourselves. I was that girl as well.

I was the go-to for all of the advice, counseling, and comfort. I freely poured into others. I was their rescue friend. You know who they are. Never is there a time that you will find them saying, "No." Always available. Always wearing a smile. Always putting my best foot forward. But eventually, that ran out. Being the "nice girl" certainly gets old and always ended up making me feel less-than when these friends moved on to the next thing.

During those years, I really don't recall the details personally, but our family quit attending church. Strangely, I barely noticed it. But it happened. I suppose it was right after I married husband number 1 because I got married in the church we attended. I graduated high school in June, got married in July and Hurricane Hugo smashed into our lives in September 1989.

GROWING UP: The "Normal" Years

I was living in a house with my new husband where the backyard was within walking distance to his children's mother's best friend's yard. On top of that, she was staying there as well due to the storm. We also had his brother, mother and sister staying with us to ride out the storm, and they never left. Their home was destroyed, so I was stuck in that house—newly married with a house full of family. That wouldn't have been so bad, except his family really didn't want me in their family. They wanted the ex in the picture. There was *a lot* of drama that I won't get into in this book. But that was something that we never got past. I moved out of there and pretty quickly into yet another dysfunctional relationship.

I moved to Alabama with the next man in my life. Alcohol and pot were just a normal thing—and so were the fights. He actually shot a hole in the kitchen ceiling one night and that was it for me. I headed back to South Carolina.

I then met my first heavy drug addict "boyfriend." I ended up stranded in Georgia with him. I had no clue who owned the house we stayed in, and that started a downward spiral. I knew this was not where I belonged, good self-esteem or not. It was just ignorant to stay in that place, knowing no one. I had to get my best friend to help me get home from that one, and I was so grateful. Thankfully, she asked no questions. She just wired me the money.

Throughout this time, I actually was lucky enough to land some decent jobs with my high school diploma, but none that would stick. I had office experience so I spent decades working in various administrative positions. I would generally thrive in my job, but inevitably, it would end. Nothing seemed permanent.

I then married the father of my children. There was not a romantic proposal of any sort. But there is indeed a story, so I will tell it, as I recall it.

I was introduced to him by my sister—who was dating his cousin. This was actually the day he was released from prison. I thought he was really good looking and fun. The first night we hung out, we drank Everclear liquor. That should have been my sign that this wasn't good. There wasn't really any sort of courting. We just partied together. I had a car and was cool enough to hang out with, especially since he really had nothing else to do.

This "friendship" was one that created our first child. He was only out of prison for a short time before he got arrested again because he was an alcoholic and drug addict. When I was three months pregnant with our first child, he went to prison once again for a year.

My son Michael was born while his father was incarcerated, and their first meeting was held in a South Carolina penitentiary, barely a week after his birth. I traveled quite a distance and it really broke my heart. I wrote to him every single day. I even visited around Christmas time and my baby and I spent Christmas dinner alone in a Chinese restaurant in a strange town. Again, there were significant clues everywhere, right?

GROWING UP: The "Normal" Years

When Michael was about three months old, his father was released. At the time, he was addicted to crack cocaine as well as alcohol, and he was ill-equipped for parenthood. However, less than a year later, we conceived my daughter. Since we would soon have two children, we decided to get married. He literally did it for the party after the wedding. Anyone who was there, knows how well that turned out. It was the beginning of a marriage that would be filled with many more nights just like that one.

Let's just say, for the next 13 years, we would continue to struggle because we were united in the most divided way possible. There's a reason why God instructs us to be "equally yoked." The only bond between us was our children at this point, and yet, we were entering into "wedded bliss."

You see, I thought I could "fix" him. I thought that if I just loved him enough, he would reciprocate the love, affection and adoration I had for him. Instead, I began to resent him. If you can't accept a person 100% for who they are the day you marry them, don't expect that you can change them. You may compliment them. You may empower them. You may encourage them. But no one can change another person. True change only comes from Christ and a life devoted to continued self-development in all areas of your own life.

CHAPTER 2
Sister Christian

Or So I Thought...

You would think I could recall exactly when I got back into church, but I can't. As I'm sure you realize by now, there are many holes in my memories. But, I'll share what I can recall. This chapter will cover the years I was married to the father of my children and the rise and fall of my seven-year Christian walk during that marriage.

While I tell my story, my truth, I'm also being mindful not to tell any more about him (or anyone else) than is necessary to share my truths. I write this so others will know that awful times can and will happen, not to hurt anyone who was involved. We can all rise above and make changes that last a lifetime.

After my children's father and I got married, we lived in a very old house in the middle of town. Rent was only $100 a month and it was where we would bring our little girl home from the hospital. My oldest was as smart as a whip and *full* of energy. He was two and we had a newborn. These were our first two children. One boy and one girl. We would go on to have two more boys later in life together. All of my children belong to him.

When I met their father, he had already been entangled in drug and alcohol abuse since he was about 11 years old. He was 18 when we met and I was 21. We obviously didn't have a romantic encounter that created a life-long bond of love and affection.

We got past the prison years for him and he would sporadically make enough of an attempt to seem like he was getting help, without actually getting clean. It started with AA meetings and I even went to Al-Anon. That didn't go well. It just wasn't my thing—or his. I definitely didn't feel like I fit in there at all. It was simply another one of the "negotiations" we made in an effort to resolve the addictions. Unfortunately, it did not work.

The drug-use ramped up and the alcoholism increased. So, another negotiation was that I would buy three cases of beer and then we didn't have to go to the store several times a week. Boy, oh boy, was that a very bad idea. Needless to say, those three cases never even came close to lasting for the week. It was Pandora's Box.

You see, I was constantly trying to control and manage him and the addictions he was battling. This was impossible. He would quickly regain control by going to the store, and wouldn't return for hours or even days. That question he asked before leaving, if I needed anything, became something I would remember forever. I guess it's a good thing I never really "needed" anything.

SISTER CHRISTIAN: Or So I Thought...

We split up multiple times and would reunite with a new plan to work things out. We did manage to split up for about a year and then got back together; that was the longest separation. I would toss him out, he would get to the bottom, come back and we would continue that cycle for years to come. It was a total and constant power struggle.

After that long separation, we moved into my grandmother's old trailer that I had bought from my uncle and mom. It was pretty nice and I loved having memories of her around me. After some time, we moved the trailer to the land my parents lived on. It's still the property we live on today. That old trailer is intact and my middle son now lives there.

If this house could talk, it would tell so many stories. I will share a few. After we moved, it was like a fresh start. I thought, "This is it." He loved my family as his own and we were all close. However, he always wanted me to cling to him and not be quite so close to them, which I also tried. That had no effect either.

There were good times. There were family things that we did and enjoyed. We shared many family meals. We were blessed with two more boys. We would sing and play music as a family. We would have fun outside. It wasn't all bad. The potential is what kept me hanging on to the marriage.

My parents have been married for 56 years. I wanted what they had. This man was the father of my children and we had so much potential. Unfortunately, addiction would be the tool used by Satan to utterly destroy our family and forever create a division that would have irreparable consequences. Of course, I attempted to try to manage *his* addiction, while being completely oblivious to my own.

What next? I had tried 12-step programs, negotiating what and where he could drink, loving him when he was absolutely unlovable, and still nothing. Next up, Jesus. I saw what prayer had done for my family in the past. I mean, hey, if God could heal my father from being a diagnosed paranoid schizophrenic, surely he could deliver my husband, the father of my children, from a life of drug and alcohol addiction. Therefore, I decided to start going to church.

Actually, I tried several churches. Eventually, I found the one. This amazing group of people will always be near and dear to my heart. They were in a church that believed in a theory that they referred to as "double married." According to this theory, I was living in a state of unforgivable sin with my children's father, my husband, at the time. So, I began to theorize right back at them. "Let me get this straight, I can murder husband #1 and then I am 'legal' in the eyes of Christ with husband #2, and that is forgiven? What? No way. That could not be the God I served."

With that stalemate, which I couldn't reconcile, I was led to search for other churches that would be more aligned with my beliefs. As everyone who knows me can tell you, belief is everything to me.

I grew up with what my family and I refer to as a "Bapticostal" background. That is one-part Baptist and the other part Pentecostal Holiness. I still hold most of these beliefs near and dear to my heart. Although I had strayed, I was genuinely saved at the young age of 11 and baptized with my best friend, Vicki. I don't believe that I ever lost my salvation. The reason I believe this so strongly is that the Holy Spirit never left me. I still continued to feel conviction and discernment, and I just knew He was still there.

I couldn't bring my high-spirited children to my family's low-key Baptist church for fear of them literally causing mass destruction. They were a busy crew, indeed. So, I searched for a more lively church. In my search, I knew that I had found "my people." It was a little country church that also was filled with other lively children. The folks there were just down to earth and friendly. They loved to sing, and so did I. My kids have always had a love for music as well. Honestly, it was just a natural progression due to both of their parents sharing a love for music.

Their dad would go on to learn the guitar and play and sing in church. I would sing along with music and he would say, "Who sings that song?" I swiftly responded with a name and he replied, "Then, why don't you let them sing it?" and then laughed at me. He intended it as a joke. That is just the way he is with humor. But I took it as he didn't think I could sing. It literally cut me to the core.

Once I got involved in church again, I returned to something I've always loved—playing the piano. Although I had definitely never mastered it, I always dreamed of being able to play anything I wanted. But in spite of my limitations, I always loved it.

I would play the piano when my heart was hurt, and it was a positive outlet. It would encourage me and fill my soul. It was how I coped with my pain. This little church welcomed my tiny talent and made me feel like I was something special. I even started writing songs, as did my husband. My dearest friend Farris led the whole bandwagon of encouragement. I'm still close with her to this day, and she'll never understand the impact she had on my life.

I began to step up to sing and play special songs for the congregation. In a country church, that's when you basically get your moment on stage to share a talent the Lord has given you. I was super nervous, and it took all I had to get through it. I used to sing in church as a young child. That's where I would begin to embrace the talent God had given me. I was always utterly terrified, but my passion for it would override my fear.

It wasn't very long until I found myself led right into ministry. Little old me ended up becoming the church choir leader. I worked with the youth and the choir. I was the youngest member, and boy, did I learn being in the music ministry could be rewarding. It was also a huge point of attack by Satan. I mean, let's be honest, in biblical times when battles were fought, they sent the musicians to the frontline. Who could have known that the thing I loved dearly would be the thing that would drive me away?

I was devout. The children and I would go to church every

Sunday morning, Sunday night and Wednesday night. When revival opened up, we went every night. I was on fire for Jesus. I prayed and read my Bible every single night. But I didn't just read the Bible, I studied the Bible. It was what I poured all of my effort into.

We prayed over meals. We prayed for their daddy. We prayed for the sick. We prayed a lot. I discovered my children all had a gift for prayer. They had a heart for it. Once my oldest son and I were on our knees in the living room praying. It was a night their father hadn't come home. We prayed like never before. Later that night, their father came home and told me a story that I'll never forget. He said that he was at the dope man's house and out of nowhere, this man pulled a gun on him, pointed it at his head and pretty much told him he needed to go home. I told him we had prayed for him.

I would get cloths anointed and put them in his boots. I would lay hands on him and pray for him in his sleep. I would go to the front of the church, completely distraught and crying out to God, I would "cover" him in prayer. I wanted so much for him to be saved. You see, I thought that was the final solution. I thought, if only my husband would get saved, it would fix it all. We had a beautiful family and I simply adored him. That is, when I was not resenting him or trying to change him.

Well, my, my, my, after my persistent pestering, he did begin to go to church with me and the kids. Eventually, he got saved. These amazing people, whom I loved so much, embraced him fully. They even encouraged him to sing and learn the guitar.

He came from a father who was naturally super-talented in music. The fruit didn't fall far from the tree. He shifted from the drinking songs of George Jones over to the gospel songs of George Jones. He learned three chords on that guitar and it was on. He loved the spotlight as well. He thrived in it. We even began to use music as our enjoyment together at home. I played the piano; he played the guitar. Then, he began to learn some on the piano as well.

Everything should have been amazing at this point, right? Well, it would have been. However, I had been so busy praying for him and revolving my whole life around him getting saved, that I hadn't worked enough on myself. To my surprise, things were not all rainbows and unicorns.

Then what happened? I'll tell you. My insecurities shifted into high gear. I felt more inferior and irrelevant than ever. He was thriving and shifted with ease to the spotlight. Unfortunately, I didn't like that one bit. Due my lack of support, it became even more difficult for him. I'd been in church for seven years, and now I had to make room for him. I had to decrease so he could increase. I found that I was very ill-equipped to do so.

He began to slip back into the old ways and would use. He would go on drug binges. He would borrow money from the church people. I was embarrassed. I was hurt. I was mad. But I was also so full of arrogance and pride that I hurt him more than I helped him. I think I wanted him to feel inferior like me. I wanted his confidence. I was jealous of the attention he got. I was jealous of how it was all so easy for him.

I decided to punish him. I decided to try to make him feel inferior. I chose the wrong way, and it was so far from godly that I can't even relate to that person anymore. No wonder I fell away from Christ. I got so far off point that I couldn't even see what should have been abundantly clear to me. I loved him, don't get me wrong. But I certainly *did not* love myself. I didn't value the person that God created me to be. I didn't value the life and the abundance that God had blessed me with in any manner. This ungrateful attitude was the beginning of our demise.

The Scripture that comes to mind is "As a man thinks, so is he." I ended up thinking myself right into not even going to church. I thought myself into being angry at the church. I thought myself into destroying my position as church choir leader. I thought myself into getting gastric bypass. I was so lost. The next big fix was on the horizon. If only I could lose the weight.

Do you see a pattern emerging? It was always "the next thing." It was always the next thing that would make me happy. It would always be an excuse that I ultimately used to stay stuck in the same place. Well, if such and such happened, everything would just be so much better. I could not be happy in the moment. I had no gratitude for the blessings I was receiving. Why would God give me more? I was never happy. I just could not live in the moment.

I ditched the Christian walk and picked up some smokes, a six pack of beer and began working towards getting gastric bypass. As a man thinks, right? Well, of course, I got gastric bypass.

The order of events is so foggy in my mind that I can only share snapshots of what happened at various points in time. Please bear with me as I attempt to unwrap this love story, if you will.

The resentment that he began to store up, I believe, resulted in him creating an environment that taught my kids that I did not matter and that they didn't need to listen to me. This was a daily struggle for me, especially considering that ADD/ADHD was a pretty prevalent characteristic in my children already.

They watched me work harder on trying to fix him, while feeling ever so inferior about myself. I always put myself last. This made me resentful as well. Unfortunately, it became a cycle. And a very unhappy one at that. I just couldn't find my way to any kind of solution.

I would try to be the devout wife, of course. I homeschooled the kids, of which he highly disapproved. I had dinner on the table between 6 and 7pm each night, which was definitely optional for him to attend. It all just seemed to be a game of cat and mouse. As "devout" as I attempted to be, I could also be a "Petty Betty," trying to be the boss of him, belittling him and putting him down. For these things, I must take responsibility. Broken relationships are never one person's fault. Period.

I wanted him to love me, but in retrospect, that was just never going to happen. He had his own demons to face—but, that's his story to tell. In my experience, you can't truly love anyone until you have the love of Christ in your life. No other love can compare to this love. You cannot give what you do not have.

I must say that we were young. Raising four children in a dysfunctional home is nearly impossible. But there were good times. There were memories to be cherished. There was a form of love in our home. It just was too weak to survive the addictions and insecurities that wreaked havoc in our lives. Little did we know, the worst was yet to come.

To this day, I don't recall exactly what happened to cause us to leave the church, but we did. He decided he was done with church and I figured why bother with it myself? We just couldn't get it together. Maybe if we had stayed in church, our stories would have a different ending. But of course, that's not how this story goes.

I thought I was fat. I thought I was unloved. I thought I wasn't good enough. I thought that if maybe I cleaned house better, it would have saved us. But let's be honest, it was very tough—trying to clean up after four kids while working and homeschooling—combined with a husband who refused to help. It just wasn't a winning combination.

Through all of this, I made a full circle around once again, to the next good thing that would radically change my life. My new answer was gastric bypass surgery. I reached an all-time high of 364.5 pounds and got approved. I thought this was it. I thought things were about to change. I thought I was all set to be super successful because I was finally going to achieve overcoming my biggest challenge: my weight.

Little did I understand the extra pounds were simply a manifestation of what was going on in my mind. I was an emotional eater, and gastric bypass could not fix that. Food was my friend. Food was my comfort. Food didn't discourage me, talk back, or judge. Food was always my go-to. Even now as I write this book, I am snacking on a low-carb candy bar.

You see, I did not eat out of necessity or hunger. I ate to celebrate. I ate to mourn. I ate when I was bored. I ate when we had family gatherings. I ate at church events. I just ate. This destructive behavior had me at an all-time high on the scale. Eating is still something I work on daily, especially when my emotions kick in. However, thanks to ketones, I am able to keep a positive mindset and work through these victories at a rate of 1% better every single day. I don't have to do it perfect. Likely, in the writing of this book, I'll add a few pounds. But that's okay, it won't last forever.

All of these thoughts led me to a moment in time that would most certainly change my life in a radical way. But not exactly how I envisioned it. First and foremost, it was not something I prayed about and felt led to do. It was not because of some major health issue. It was a purely selfish act. I just wanted to be skinny. I didn't care if it shaved years off my life. I just wanted in on this skinny girl journey.

The surgery was all paid for with the exception of $300 for a psychological evaluation. In my personal opinion, this surgery did something to the chemistry in my brain. But of course, I'm not a doctor and can't confirm this. It's simply a theory.

I went to Anderson, South Carolina, to get my surgery done. I had researched and it seemed the best choice for me. Later, my uncle and sister would follow my example. I was following my best friend in hers. I was sick of being a fat girl.

It was degrading. The scale alone was just beyond belief. I couldn't even weigh at home any longer. I tipped it at an all-time high of 364.5 pounds and that was right before my surgery.

The surgery was done laparoscopically—meaning that they didn't need to make a large incision. I thought I was fully prepared for what was about to come. Sadly, I was not.

Straight out of surgery, I didn't feel any different, of course. The exception being that I could no longer eat. I was limited to a liquid diet. My parents had taken me for the procedure, an outpatient procedure with a post-surgical plan I hadn't prepared for. We checked into a hotel that was close by for me to stick around and wait until my checkup.

I'm not sure how long we were there. Maybe a few days. But I do recall being an angry bird right off the rip. I had two tubes that came from my stomach and were hanging on my sides. On top of that, I was surrounded by those who loved me, but they also still had to eat. They cared for me, of course. But they didn't realize that bringing Chinese food back to the room would set me off. Wow! I thought to myself, what have I done? I couldn't eat any of it, except for the egg drop soup. Wow! This was amazing. But I couldn't believe this was my irreversible life. Liquid only.

We had to go back to the office for one final checkup before heading home (which was four hours away) to continue my recovery. When I went back, it was time to remove those tubes. I'll never forget the feeling of these tubes. It was like snakes were crawling out of my belly. I felt sick.

As I recall, on the trip home, I had some mashed potatoes from KFC. I also recall a phone conversation with my bestie, Lyn Dell. I was like, "I think you lied to me. This is hard." Anyone who tells you gastric bypass is a shortcut, the easy way out, is absolutely an absurd liar. There was no turning back, but in my opinion, it was anything but easy.

Once I got home, I learned I could drink protein shakes as well as puree anything I wanted. One little creation I made was steak and asparagus. I had to relearn eating. I could eat about a tablespoon at a time.

I want to remind you that I had a head problem, not a stomach problem. So, my mind began to embrace all the things I could do. As you can imagine, I wasn't great at following rules anyway. Now, this leg of my journey was to begin.

The first six months were really tough. I was down about 100 pounds and looked like death. Keep in mind, that put me at about the weight I am currently. I still felt fat. But others began to notice my weight loss, so that encouraged me. At this point, it wasn't so much work anymore, it was a lifestyle. I learned what foods would make me throw up. I learned what foods would make me "dump," which means get horribly sick. I learned all the things.

There were still rules I didn't follow. I didn't drink water like I should have. I didn't take vitamins like I should have. I didn't eat protein at first like I should have. I would also eat foods that were high in calories and horrible for me. Let's just say, if you can only eat a small amount of food, it should not be potato chips, which went down really easy, as opposed to that baked chicken.

I was still the same person. I just began to transform on the outside. I had left church, so I had no support there. As I shared earlier, I had picked up smoking and drinking—two things they had specifically warned against. As a matter of fact, either of those would have disqualified me from getting the surgery.

Adding these two beauties to my life would swiftly take me to a whole new level, a whole new crowd of people. My husband and I were both drinking and smoking and he was doing his drugs. I was actually angrier than ever. I was angry at God. Wow. Really? I mean, I created all of this with my decisions. How could I be angry at God? It's just non-sensical, right? But in my mind, it all made perfect sense.

I met new friends. These friends would ultimately be the friends who introduced me to drugs and a plethora of bad decisions. But they weren't responsible for those decisions. Obviously, they were not to blame. I put myself into this space. I don't even recall how we met. Likely it was at a bar or through a mutual friend.

I recall going to bars and getting attention—attention I had never gotten before, and I liked it. I actually felt beautiful. I had gotten down to a size 8 and was down 200 pounds. But in my mind I was still the fat girl. I still *felt* overweight. My body still felt bad. But I did get a high from the attention I got. I looked mighty fine in clothes—I have to admit.

I thought to myself, this will get his attention. If other men want me, that will make him want me more. But the only thing that really happened was more time for him to do his thing, and I began to do mine. The distance in our relationship grew ever-greater and we drifted further apart than we had ever been.

We occasionally used drugs together as well. I figured, can't beat 'em, join 'em, right? Wrong. That was a bad move on my part. It also distanced us even more. Ultimately, this surgery was the point of no return. I felt like I could do "better." I felt like I would find someone else.

Turns out, he moved on after our divorce quite easily. I, however, did not. You see, I didn't file for divorce because I wanted a divorce. I filed for divorce because I wanted *him* to see *me*. To notice *me*. To give me the attention I so desperately wanted in my life. I was trying to use him to fill the space that only God could fill. I was trying to get him to complete me. In essence, that was completely unfair to him. It was not *his* responsibility to be for me what I could not be for *myself.*

The court date for the divorce arrived, and he didn't even bother to show up. I was devastated. But why? I was the one who had filed for divorce. You see, we need to say what we mean, and mean what we say. The moment I filed, it was over. There was no turning back.

It was at this point of feeling rejected once again that I began to go deeper into the lost life I was pursuing. This, quite honestly, was the beginning of the end. This is where the alter-ego that I would build for myself was born. This was the moment in time that I felt things shift radically. We refer to this time frame as the evolution of "Malenka." In the next chapter, you'll get to know the new personality I created in an effort to erase the person whom God created me to be. It's in this the part of the book that I'll share those things that ultimately led me to prison.

CHAPTER 3
Malenka likes to Drinka
The Plot Thickens

After the divorce, I felt lost. For 13 years, my identity was attached to this man and my children. It was now being dissolved to a point that the memories would fade with each passing day. No one likes change, right? I was no different. Somehow, I held onto the notion that he would see what he was missing and return to me, as he had done so many times before. Turns out, that would never happen. I recall the exact place I was when he told me I might as well move on because he was in love with his new girlfriend.

In that very moment, she became my number one enemy. I completely despised her, and I embarked on years of making a fool of myself and acting ridiculous toward this woman. It was not her fault that our marriage failed. She was never to blame for what didn't exist in my life. That honor strictly belonged to me. Yet, I was in complete denial.

She was much younger and was absolutely gorgeous. I felt even more inferior than ever. She had it all together, of course. Every hair was in its place. Perfect makeup, perfect job, perfect everything. She also only had one child, who adored his soon-to-be stepfather.

I mean, wow, what's not to love, right? I knew I had lost him. She did all the things I used to do. She took care of business. She was a leader. She took charge. I didn't appreciate any of that at the time. I was filled with jealousy and envy for the life I no longer had as an option. She was now living the life I felt I should have had. Yet, as I looked at my own life, it became more and more bleak.

Because of my mindset at the time, it became my mission to replace him as swiftly as possible. I found myself on Match.com website looking for "the one." I ended up going on a date with a man I met through this internet connection. But, prior to accepting, he had some convincing to do. He had three strikes against him right out the gate. His name was the same as my kids' father's. He was Catholic. Not to mention, he was *much* shorter than me. But, after much persuasion, I agreed to a first date.

We had a great time. He paid for dinner and we talked for hours. I had never had someone be so attentive to my every word. It was refreshing. We went out quite often after that and we instantly became a couple. He lavished me with flowers and surprises. He rented a limousine one year for my birthday. He was even going to take me to Hawaii. Sounds perfect, right? Well, that's what I had led everyone to think.

We hit the bars hard. We were a very social and charismatic

MALENKA LIKES TO DRINKA: The Plot Thickens

couple. Everyone loved us and wanted to be around us. I came out of my shell and was the life of the party. You know that part where sin seems fun for a season? This was that season.

The drinking became intense and daily. I had been dabbling in some drug use as well. It was no big deal. After all, it did nothing for me. I was prescribed Adderall for my ADD and I didn't hesitate to use it recreationally. We learned how to snort it for the added effect of staying awake. Again, this was no big deal. It was prescribed, after all.

It wasn't long after that my job performance began to suffer. The drinking and the drugs were becoming a huge hindrance for me. Ultimately, I ended up losing a job I had held for 5 years. It was a job I loved. I did leave on decent terms, though, and finished out what was asked of me. However, they gave me a really horrible reference, which stalled me in my career path.

I had started a business working for myself as a financial manager/consultant for small businesses while I had the other job. Then after I quit, I just filled the time with these side jobs, which was great at first. However, when an economic disaster hit the US, the first jobs to go were those in my category.

The job hunt began. I did my research and found two markets that didn't seem to be affected—Walmart and cell phone companies. So, I went that direction. By this time, I had married the man I met on Match.com. Oh, I guess I should share the fact my kids' father had planned to marry the woman I referenced previously, so that I would marry this man was pretty much a given. I knew it wasn't the right thing to do, but I ended up doing it anyway.

Why was I hesitant to marry? Why did he have to propose more than once? Well, there were secrets. Obviously, writing this book will bring some of those to light. Again, let me state, this is not meant to harm anyone. This man and I remain friends to this day. We just didn't make a great couple. He was the jealous type. Insecurities plagued him as well, just like me. This would be what ultimately divided us. It got ugly. It got really, really ugly. We can't go back in time and I'm not going to share all of the details. But I will share a few to help you better understand what happened.

We had the house. It was the nicest house I had ever lived in. I kept it spotless. We had the charisma. We looked on the surface like the perfect couple. We both worked. We were fun.

He was smart. He was funny. He was handsome. But he was not my kids' father. My children never took to him. They knew what happened behind closed doors and just couldn't accept it all. This marriage would not endure for so many reasons.

He would also hop around from job to job as well, due to the excessive drinking. He wasn't into the drugs. But boy could he drink. He was also pretty good at playing pool. We would take the bars by storm. They all knew us. When we walked in, the fun had arrived. Except for when it didn't.

MALENKA LIKES TO DRINKA: The Plot Thickens

That's when the arguments would come into play. He had an anger issue. He had an issue with being addicted to the argument. I had an issue with losing all of who I was. The person he thought he knew doesn't even exist. She was a fictional character that I had created.

I recall hiding bruises with makeup. As a matter of fact, one year I made my Halloween costume to fit with the black eye. I ended up taking a part time job at Walmart and ended up quitting because I couldn't cover things up there. The employees there were simply too nosey and would definitely mind your business for you.

The next job was AT&T. I recall huge bouquets being sent to me in an attempt to gain my forgiveness for the abuse. He was genuinely remorseful. But honestly, he just couldn't help it. He had anger brewing inside of him that had nothing to do with me. And so it really didn't matter what I did, it was not going to pan out.

We ended up being evicted from that amazing house. The lifestyle we lived couldn't hold up. I don't quite remember exactly how we split or when. But I do recall that my house was no longer a home, and once again, it all fell to pieces.

But admitting defeat? Failure? All while their father and his new bride were living the dream? No way. I continued to put on a happy face. We ended up living in an apartment once again.

My daughter was sickly and out on homebound with school. She helped with the little ones a lot. My oldest was mischief, but not a bad kid at heart. I became an absent mom. It felt like I was almost required to go out nightly. I began to feel so much guilt as a mother. Yet, I was torn. Because of this inner battle, my self-esteem was getting worse and worse.

The weight began to slowly creep back on. The drinking would prove to be a big part of my weight gain. That's when I switched from drinking beer to liquor. Having gastric bypass, I learned I could get drunk quickly and get sober quickly—and I did it several times a day. That, combined with the pills, created more anger and bigger issues. Ultimately, one day a massive fight ensued. I ended up with a black eye, and for the first time, I lashed back out against him in self-defense and broke his nose.

That was on the eve of his trip to Hawaii for work. I refused to go. Although he had to go, his father was left behind to contend with me. I felt that if I left the house, I wouldn't be able to get back in to get any of my things. His dad had a key and came into the house while I was there. I knew I was being painted as the bad guy. In all honesty, at this point in our lives, we were both the bad guys. We were simply two people who were broken and trying to find something, anything, to gain any sense of a happy life.

Of course, we eventually mended things while he was still out of town. He returned from Hawaii with a special gift for me, as he always did on his trips around the world. It was a keychain. On one side, it said Marsha. On the other was the Hawaiian name for

MALENKA LIKES TO DRINKA: The Plot Thickens

Marsha—"Malenka." I actually think it was Maleka. But saying it out loud, it turned into Malenka. That would end up being shortened to "Lenka."

It was a fun game. We went to bars and began to introduce me as "Malenka." People would go on and on about how they loved that name. So, we gave him one as well. His Hawaiian name was "Keoni." But, he definitely could not pull off a "Keoni." So we went with an English name, "Zayne." At any rate, it became this huge thing. Oh look: "Hey! It's Zayne and Malenka."

Our marriage lasted about a year. But our friendship has continued for over a decade. As a matter of fact, he was my only visitor when I went to prison. For that, I will be eternally grateful. We remain friends to this day. I don't blame him. We all have our own demons to face. I do know it was not personal against me. I pray he knows that I have a love for him and cherished memories—even through the bad times.

After the divorce, I eventually remarried. Once again, I was on the hunt for "the one." The one who would save me from it all. The one who would help me be a better me. I decided to hit the bars again—a single mom of four who was well down the road of alcoholism and just beginning the journey of drug addiction. Sure enough, I found husband number four.

We met on the night of Father's Day. Admittedly, I was interested in his friend, which, in retrospect, was an even bigger mess, of course. Thankfully, that did not work out. I was graciously passed off to his buddy, as we engaged in a game of pool in a bar that was mostly empty.

He was military. Relatively good looking. Clean cut and seemed nice enough. On paper, it seemed he would've been the perfect match. We began dating. However, I ended up being hidden for months because, you see, he was in the middle of a divorce, and it was not pretty. He didn't handle confrontation well at all. And, because I felt the need to be supportive of his needs, I ended up hidden in the shadows.

First of all, ladies, if you must be hidden, you're not where you need to be. Period. That should have been a red flag from early on. Secondly, I should have been able to just enjoy a brand new, developing relationship. But we had to sneak around. I was not spoken of or introduced to friends or family. This made me feel pretty less-than. This went on for months.

Meanwhile, I'm telling all of my friends and family about this invisible man in my life. He was close to retirement. He had an outstanding service record. He adored his mother. I thought, this is the one. My kids even liked him, at first. Furthermore, my parents liked him too, and they had not liked anyone I had ever dated. Eventually, his divorce was finalized.

I had been working at AT&T and things were not going well there at all. I had an employee who wanted my spot, as he was only part time, and he was dead set on getting me out of the way. I had some medical issues, and combining the two, I ended up needing to leave the job. I also was in the middle of being evicted due to medical bills and being out of work.

At the same time, this man whom I thought was the one, had the end of his apartment lease coming up. Several times I broached the subject. He kept putting me off. To me, it didn't make any sense to pay rent on two places while he was mostly staying at mine, or I at his. Reluctantly, we temporarily moved our stuff into his apartment. I really had nowhere else to go, except back home to the country. I was adamant that I did not want to return to that old trailer under any circumstances.

We lived together from June to October. He finally did ask me to marry him, but it wasn't really anything to write home about. He did at least have a ring. I could tell he really didn't want to, but financially it was a good move for him. He was retiring and this would give him more income. After all, it was the four children and me. Each dependent would bring in more money. Not to mention, he no longer had any housing expenses to speak of by moving into my paid-for trailer.

We went on our honeymoon to his mom's house in Connecticut. That was a bit strange, but I agreed. It was decent. I did all I could to win over his friends and family. But they didn't care for me much at all. He was Portuguese and spoke it with others, so it was easy for him to discuss details without me knowing things. Actually, as it turns out, he was a very secretive person, and for years to come, would live in a space of deception.

After we married, we moved into my trailer. It was paid for and he could hoard even more money. It seemed our marriage was only created out of his need for more money and the ability to spend it how he chose. I had no say in anything financial. He hid many things from me. He had to hide it because he did not want me to spend any of *his* money.

The following month, he retired, technically speaking. Once we were married, he didn't need to return because of all of the leave he had built up. When he retired, he had set his mind on making sure he would be able to collect 100% on disability. He was already on a plethora of medications for anxiety, headaches, PTSD, and lots of other things. I actually think he was a hypochondriac. At any rate, he followed it all to perfection and in order to not be caught in a lie, he ended up becoming 100% disabled. It was horrible.

Day in and day out, he would do nothing. He slept, watched TV, played on the computer, ate and repeated it all. His weight got totally out of control as well. On top of that, we would engage in some pretty heavy drinking. The only places we went were to my friend's house and the bars. Eventually, he even quit going with me to those. He became a complete recluse. He wouldn't do anything around the house. He was just completely lost and unmotivated for life in general. Amazon.com seemed to be his best friend. All of the

MALENKA LIKES TO DRINKA: The Plot Thickens

extra money he got for me and the kids, he would either hide or spend. His spending was out of control. But that's what seemed to make him happy.

We didn't travel. We barely went out to eat. He just sat in that house the majority of the time. It was awful. It was around this time that I began to use meth "recreationally." By this, I mean, I didn't buy it, I just used it when my friend would have it. She introduced me to it. She portrayed it as no big deal.

We were very close friends. We shared lots of secrets. This was one of them. We drank booze all the time. Rarely did we not have alcohol. Every event we participated in involved alcohol—a lot of alcohol.

As time progressed, we became more active and involved in the drugs. At first, it was mostly snorting the Adderall, maybe a bit of cocaine. But this was certainly a gateway to meth. It wasn't long before it was every time we were together that we would do it. It was cheap and it helped us sober up after drinking too much—which was pretty often. You see, doing the meth enabled us to drink more because it somehow cancelled out the effects of the booze.

By this time, I was working from home for an online company and I started to dabble in working as a deejay. That was when the name got shortened to "DJ Lenka." I played in most of the small-time bars. I was outgoing enough and it provided me even more hookups for the drugs as well as free drinks. Most of the time, until closer to the end, it supplied drinks for both me and my husband. Well, I take that back. It was my basic beer and we would buy shots to sustain the night. We regularly got completely wasted.

The friend I was always with already knew me as "Marsha." It seemed to annoy her that I had taken on this new identity. It seemed to bother her almost a little too much—like she was jealous about the attention it got me. She would regularly bring me down by screaming "Marsha" across the bars and letting everyone know who I really was quite often. It was like she felt the need to disempower me. Granted, the identity was ridiculous. But it was my choice. Who was she to call the shots on my choices? I'm guessing this was simply because of her own lack of self-worth. Let's be honest. Anyone who is consuming massive amounts of booze and drugs is not exactly living a happy life. But I'm not here to judge her, by any means. She was my friend. I trusted her.

As time went on, I got worse. Because I worked as a deejay, I began to have more access to the drugs. I built a very close relationship with a drug dealer and eventually agreed to let my house be the place where the dope was made. Prior to that, we would just hang out at my place and drink.

My husband was in state of complete misery and so was I. On top of that, we began to fight. One of the deal-breakers I introduced from day one was that I refused to have marathon arguments and nothing was worth fighting over that much. He agreed. However, that agreement had now disappeared. He only wanted to berate me.

MALENKA LIKES TO DRINKA: The Plot Thickens

He would pick apart my every move. Nothing I did was right. We began to despise each other. I would leave the house and not come home or I would sleep in the yard in my truck or at the end of the road. We lived in my house, yet I felt I had nowhere to go. I was stuck.

I would continue to push the envelope. I honestly wanted him to leave. My family no longer cared for him. He betrayed me by cheating on me with a family member, and my children had distanced themselves from him. It was time for a change, for sure.

Eventually, I returned home from a deejay gig to find that he had moved out. We had no conversation about it at all. As a matter of fact, he even refused to communicate with me on any level. He took what he wanted and left what he couldn't take. If he had the means, I know that he would have taken every single thing including my truck. Fortunately, that did not happen.

It was probably a year before we even spoke a word to each other. He just refused to do anything. It's been about six years now and we still remain married. I guess the only reason I haven't severed the tie is the health and auto insurance benefits. He pays a small portion of my auto insurance and provides his health benefits to me through Tricare. In exchange, he has collected benefits on all of my children and me for years.

It still irritates him to send me that money every month for auto insurance. I don't make him pay it because I need it. Rather, I enforce him paying it because he's receiving money for me and my children and I don't feel it's right for him to do that.

This is a marriage that still needs to be dissolved. It's my prayer that by the time you read this that my divorce will not only be filed, but it will be finalized. It's the last tie to my past that needs to be severed. I think I've avoided it because of his delicate mental state, as well as my reluctance to face the past once again and revisit another failure in my relationships.

To be honest, I'm not really sure why I make him pay it because I think he owes so much more than that. To feel like you were used financially by someone and tossed away like an old shoe doesn't sit well at all. I endured mental, physical and emotional abuse during this relationship and felt like I took on all of his old baggage and it sent me over the edge. Yet, I sit here and know that I must forgive him as well as the others. I mean, really, it wasn't exactly a match made in heaven. Dissolving it is really only a formality at this point.

I did notice that once I was able to get my life on-track every single one of them have changed their view of me as well. I'm no longer the loser. The villain. The poor little screw-up. I don't need a man to validate my existence. I can stand on my own two feet. I love who I am alone. I love the person God made me to be. I love that I am thriving in every single area of my life.

I have finally discovered myself—and it feels good. But how did it all happen? When did it all happen? To be frank, there is still much to tell about this story. However, this will require yet another relationship to be shared. Because I'm still not divorced from husband number four, the next one was just a live-in situation. You want to take a guess as to where we met? You betcha! We met in a bar.

I was deejaying at a local dive bar that night. I had become a full-time drug user and alcohol was my constant companion. So out of pure boredom, I chose the only half-decent looking one in the bar that night. He was a regular and he was *loud*. He also came across to be pretty full of himself. But in retrospect, I believe he harbored his own self-esteem issues that he would never admit to. Let's call him "Derik." I had a plan to take him back to his place and then pretty much be done with him. I had zero intent on anything further than what that would mean.

Oddly enough, those qualities I portrayed seemed to be attractive to this single man when it came to a one-night stand. He continued to show interest in me. Although I was much older, he seemed to have a history of dating older woman. He was about 10 years younger than me. He seemed fun and outgoing, at the time. However, it was clear he wasn't addicted only to drinking, but also to being a daily patron at the bar. He sought the attention and spotlight to feel important.

To his credit, he was probably the best pool player I had ever met. It would be a close race between him and husband #3. But there was one thing that absolutely took me in—he danced with me. He danced with me when there was no music. It was an amazing experience. It wasn't that he was even a good dancer. It was more that I had never dated anyone who could or would dance. He was tall, which was a huge plus in his favor, and when I danced with him, it made me feel great. We were also a hit as a couple in the bars—until we weren't.

You see, he was the regular, and they knew he was up to no good on the regular. He lied and he cheated. He was searching for someone to do all of the responsible things for him and needed a partner to play mom to his daughter. I was not even equipped to raise my own children at this point, much less a four-year-old. I believe that was his biggest point of resentment toward me. I was unable to fill those particular needs that he had and that created tension between us.

He had an apartment within walking distance of the bar. Before I knew it, I was head over heels and so was he. We wanted to spend all of our time together. We talked on the phone a lot and I would drive all the way from my place over 30 minutes away almost every day to see him. I couldn't keep myself from doing it either. I had no idea why. He was charismatic.

By this time, I was working for Apple as chat support from home. I always managed to have decent jobs. But it was night shift. It was difficult to get my Adderall prescription filled and go to see the doc, so I had a friend, who happened to be a drug dealer, offer a little extra help. He would hang out at my place and I began to use meth

MALENKA LIKES TO DRINKA: The Plot Thickens

to help me work the night shift and manage my work time.

Between the poor internet connection and this new relationship, I decided to sell my trailer and move to the city to rent a trailer. I thought it was decent enough. But I soon figured out that I had moved to the not-so-good side of town. Unfortunately, I fit right in. I discovered I was the not-so-good type of person as well. The location was perfect, too. It was like seven miles from my new fella's house and the bar was about three-quarters of the way there. It was perfect for me.

The kids were older now and they were pretty much on their own. I just supplied the house and living expenses at this point. I spent a ton of time, effort, energy and money on drinking and drugs by this time and was also paying the rent.

It wasn't long before I talked the boyfriend into moving in with me to split the costs. That was a huge mistake, for sure. From that point, the drinking got more intense, as did the drug use.

We went out quite a bit. But, a lot of times, he would go without me, which is what he preferred. It gained him more attention, which was his goal in the first place. I always felt like he was a popular kid in school, but in later years, that faded and he lost his "cool kid" identity. He was more like the nerdy alcoholic that couldn't really get any roots put down.

It wasn't that he was a terrible person, per se. He was just very different from me. He actually considered himself better than me, I believe. You know, his family had a little money, so he never went without. However, he seemed to always be broke due to his habits and child support. He certainly didn't spend any money on me or my kids.

I recall that it was his birthday and we had gone to visit his parents. We drove separately and I had planned a surprise birthday party at his favorite bar. He ended up being several hours late. I suspected a fling from his old stomping grounds, which he vehemently denied. But it was pretty obvious. Why else would he drag out getting to a bar that he was always at like clockwork on any other day?

After he moved in, things continued to be rocky. He would have scratch marks on his back, and I even found nudies on his phone of this girl. He swore he didn't cheat. Funny, he is now married to this nudist. I think it's comical now. You see, she ended up getting the short end of that stick. I had broken up with him. I knew he lied. I also knew he cheated.

More than that, his excessive drinking created issues that were more unacceptable than any other form of abuse I had ever encountered. Honestly, if you are a grown man and your drinking creates a situation where it makes you incontinent on a regular basis at night when you pass out, multiple times a week, then it's definitely time to get some help. That, combined with him returning to his habit for cocaine, did him no favors. It was just a bad relationship with bad circumstances. Here I was, barely able to do what I needed for my own children or myself, and he expected me to get up with his daughter and play housemom. She was not a bad kid, but that wasn't my responsibility.

He worked a lot of nights. One particular weekend, he was at work and it was my middle son's 16th birthday, and I let him invite some friends over. Of course, my house was fully stocked with booze and beer, and that was the night that shifted the course of events for my entire future.

I was busy doing my own thing. I wasn't watching them closely, and one thing led to another. Without putting a lot detail or blame into this, I ended up being arrested for contributing to the delinquency of a minor—two counts. Two teens were taken from my home with alcohol poisoning and I was taken away in handcuffs.

My son felt like it was his fault, and blamed himself. It most certainly was not his fault. I was supposed to be an adult and watch out for him and not allow anyone to be put in harm's way. I didn't do what I should have done. This would be the charge that would ultimately put me in prison. But that would not happen until a whole year later.

The boyfriend did bail me out (with my own money, of course) and picked me up. Over the next year, everyone would assure me, it was no big deal and I would get a slap on the wrist. This couldn't have been further from the truth. Every single month, I had to be accountable and available. Yet every month it was postponed.

PRISON TO PROSPERITY WITH PURPOSE

Between the relationship, which was in a constant state of deterioration, and the pressure of court, things got progressively worse. I also underwent surgery on my elbows and hands and ended up being without a job and on workers' comp. That meant that I would be tapped out of all financial means, which made the habits all the more difficult to handle.

I ended up working odd jobs—bartender, cook—whatever I could manage. But more than anything, I had once again stepped up my drug use. By this time, my drug dealing friend had made it a bit more affordable for me to continue to feed my addiction. I supplied the house. You take care of the house and the house takes care of you. It was a place he could cook dope and bring his party girls when no one was home. And that is what we did. The kids went to their dad's every other weekend and the boyfriend worked late, and it was a sure thing for him to hit up the bar afterward. That made it a wide-open opportunity.

We lived in a drug-infested community as well, so it wasn't like we drew any additional attention to ourselves. I had ended up becoming the dope house. My body, mind and face would certainly reflect what was going on in my life. Although I thought I was hiding it, I most assuredly wasn't able to hide anything from anyone. I had scabs bursting out on my face, arms and wrists. To this day, I still bear the scars. I even had hallucinations about bugs. It was a horrible thing to experience. When your mind is convinced of something, it embraces it as fact.

Methamphetamines really do something to your mind. I believe

MALENKA LIKES TO DRINKA: The Plot Thickens

that's why my facts are off at times and timelines are fuzzy. It caused depression, anxiety and an almost complete withdrawal from public places. I became a total recluse. I recall going to a concert and being in a full-blown sweat. I could hardly even go to the grocery store. At the checkout line, I would have so much anxiety, I would begin to sweat profusely. Public settings were something I avoided as much as possible.

This was not all because of the drugs. I have a history of mental illness. I have battled with depression, anxiety, ADD and social disfunction over the years, even before the drugs and alcohol. But now, they were at the highest peak ever. I was paranoid. I was angry. I was unpredictable. Ultimately, on my daughter's 21st birthday, I even attempted suicide. By the grace of God, I survived. Let me correct that. (By the grace of God, I not only survived, but was ultimately delivered from all of this and much more—but, that I will get to that later.)

I had lost the will to live. I had lost any sense of who I was anymore. I still mourned the loss of the marriage to their father. I mourned the loss of my career. I mourned the loss of any hope for a future. My life was darker than I ever thought it could be and I detested who I had become.

I was living in every level of sin. I even cheated on my boyfriend. The paranoia was so bad that I confessed the cheating to him. Moreover, things had become so bad for me financially (and my boyfriend had refused to help) that I placed an ad on Craigslist to be a companion. I got as far as having someone come to the house—but I freaked and backed out before anything happened. I couldn't walk over that line. I would not and I did not. However, it is scary to think about how close I did get to crossing this line.

I was as unhappy as anyone could possibly be. It wasn't just my present condition. It was the culmination of everything that had happened over the course of the past 10 years. It became more than I could bear.

At that point, I had already experienced so many bad things. I felt abandoned by my church. I felt unloved and abandoned by every man I knew. I never felt I fit in with anyone, anywhere.

I had been physically, mentally and emotionally abused in a variety of ways. Black eyes. Skinned knees. Dragged by the head of my hair across a yard. Choked out while driving. Dragged out of cars onto the ground. Held under water. Deserted. Isolated. Neglected. Ignored. Taken advantage of. Lied to and lied about. Cheated on multiple times. Made fun of. Blamed. Shunned. Shamed.

I woke up soaked in urine almost on a daily basis due to my partner at the time. I was spit on. Pushed on. Slapped on. Punched on. Shoved on. I had been fired and laid off. I was turned away and turned down. I had horrible credit. I couldn't hold a job. I failed as a mother, as a daughter, as an aunt and as a Christian. All of this led me to a place where I never dreamed I would be. I had broken the law and had some very serious charges pending against me. This would haunt me daily, as I had hit this all-time low. I was forever an outcast. I felt completely abandoned, worthless and hopeless. There was nowhere for me to go from there. I had had enough and it was all too much to bear. I felt that life was no longer worth living and so I attempted suicide. I swallowed a handful of Trazadone and that's the last thing I remember.

The same son who had the party is the one who called 911 and saved my life. The boyfriend actually called on him to help and was more worried about him getting in trouble than saving my life. He really couldn't have cared less if I had died that day. And it broke something in my son.

He is actually my most sensitive child. He hates when I refer to him as that—but it's not sensitive as in "feminine." I mean sensitive as in he is in tune with the emotions and feelings of others so much that he feels them himself. He is an "empath" and he is strong. But this rocked his world. At this point, he really lost all interest in life. He was barely able to keep a job and go to school, especially after the party. But he persevered.

My daughter moved back home as well. She had also gotten entangled in a similar lifestyle herself. Her addictions continued while she lived at my house, but in secret. Our relationship was very distant. I didn't like the new her any more than she liked the new me. My family had been ripped apart at the seams.

My youngest son coped by eating. Food was his comfort. By the time I went to prison, he had almost no neck. My oldest had bounced around living different places with his girlfriend at the time, and she had just gotten pregnant with my first grandchild.

I was drunk daily. I was high daily. I was in more pain in my soul every waking moment of my life. I just cannot express enough how much this life tore me up inside and out. I lost everything. I couldn't wrap my head around it all. I mean, I wasn't a rocket scientist, but I sure wasn't stupid. How in the world did I get here?

I was the villain. Their dad was never the villain—and he and his wife became untouchable. They were placed on a pedestal. They would all meet every other weekend and make fun of the mess my life was in. Comments of multiple identities and my house being in complete chaos. Judgment. Condemnation. I really felt it hard. I was despised by everyone, or so it seemed. That killed me inside. From the moment I had ended my marriage to their father, I felt like I was the target. I was the brunt of every joke. I was the weekend comedy hour. Meanwhile, my kids kept all of their secrets from me. No bad words were ever spoken of anyone else. So, in my mind, I was the screw-up and everyone else's lives were gift-wrapped with rainbows and unicorns. I was full of resentment and hatred for them.

How dare they make fun of me? Before the divorce, I would claim that I was the picture-perfect wife. I cooked dinner. And not only did I raise the kids by myself, but I did it while he made it even harder by teaching them all to disrespect me. It just didn't seem fair to me. No matter what I did, it just never worked out. I was in one

MALENKA LIKES TO DRINKA: The Plot Thickens

mess after another. The mention of my name would never ignite any positive feelings, that's for sure. I was a horrible mess and had been for over a decade.

Oddly enough, all of this would be wiped away in one single moment. I can describe it quite simply in a few words. I felt something so deep that I had never felt before in my whole life. I felt perfect love, grace and forgiveness. I finally had the missing connection with Jesus. The things of this world that I sought took me further than I planned to go, took more from me than I planned to give, and kept me longer than I planned to stay. They could never fill that God-space that is only able to be filled with a deep, personal relationship with Jesus. Nothing, I could do on my own was worthwhile. It took Jesus to set it all in place and to live in the peace that surpasses my own understanding. That's what it took for me.

But to receive these things, I had to *ask* for them. I had been running a long time. I know the Holy Spirit was still there, but I felt like God hated me. I felt unlovable even for the Creator. But you see, there is one thing God can't do—and that is *can't*. He is a *can-do* God. His resources are unlimited. Love. Patience. Forgiveness. Everything I wanted from other people and would never get was waiting on me. I just simply needed to *ask*. The word is clear about *ask, seek, knock*.

In the Sermon on the Mount, Jesus told his disciples "Ask, and it will be given to you; seek, and you will find; knock, and the door will be opened to you. For everyone who asks receives, and he who seeks finds, and to him who knocks it will be opened" (Matthew 7:7-8).

My job was to ask, seek and knock. God's responses allowed me to receive, find and have doors opened. The first step would need to be for me to ask God for help. Yet, I wasn't ready. I still had weeks ahead before court would convene, and I kept running in circles. I kept running away from God, instead of toward Him.

The boyfriend was little or no help throughout this entire time. Not only was I fighting my own battles, I was sharing his burdens as well. Furthermore, his inability to be faithful was a huge issue, and I had zero trust in him. He definitely had much to hide, and I was not up for a game of cat-and-mouse. If my life was going to be a train wreck, fine. But I certainly wasn't going to be in a total mess along with his total mess. I believe it was about two weeks prior to me going to prison that I broke it off and asked him to move out. He was quick to comply for his own selfish reasons. Honestly, he was only there the whole time to save money to support his drinking habit. There was no love that he held for me in his heart.

During the next two weeks, the loneliness built to an all-time high. I drank more than ever and did more and more drugs. I could not bury it enough. I just couldn't numb those feelings. I couldn't grasp even the smallest amount of hope.

Honestly, I know without a doubt, God had me surrounded with angels. They protected me through all of this. I had a purpose He knew only I could fill. I was born for what was yet to come. I was a voice that would share her story, write a book, inspire and encourage many people. I bore the hurt so that I could share the forgiveness, love and grace of God. My scars would be healed and I would be delivered. I would be an ambassador for Christ.

But it did not begin in such a fantastic manner. Honestly, it all began the moment I was able to humble myself. 2 Chronicles 7:14 says, "If My people who are called by My name will humble themselves, and pray and seek My face, and turn from their wicked ways, then I will hear from heaven, and will forgive their sin and heal their land." (KJV) It was in a moment of humility that He heard me, forgave me and healed me. There was a defining moment of complete deliverance. I say this not to impress you, but to impress *upon* you, that if He did it for me, He will do it for you. You see, all of my ailments, inside and out, were healed. I no longer suffer with depression, anxiety, fear, ADD, fibromyalgia, nothing, nada. I am whole and healed. The only remaining issue I struggle with is that of emotional eating. This has always been the "thorn in my side." I imagine it always will be a struggle that reminds me that I need to "die to self" on a daily basis.

CHAPTER 4

Redeemed & Restored

All My Hope Is in Jesus

It was the day before court and I had been instructed by my lawyer to not participate in drinking or drugs before my appearance. Because I was scared they would test me, I started on Friday and I Googled exactly what I could drink and how long it would stay in my system and I was gambling on it. I am pretty sure I got really high that Friday and didn't do any more after that. It's fuzzy at best. I drank until I passed out.

By Saturday, I had reached a low in my depression. I slept as late as I could. I tried to be positive, but that was not something I could even attempt to fake at this point. It was horrible. I bargained and bantered with the Holy Spirit all night long.

Sunday morning came. I had already decided that I was going to church with my parents. You know—just in case. I dragged myself out of bed that morning. It was really hard to do. Obviously, not having the drugs, I was exhausted coming down off them. My serotonin levels were all out of whack. But I managed to get it together enough to go.

I haven't yet mentioned that my youngest, about six months before court, had moved in with my parents. He just couldn't take it anymore. He was so lost. This particular Sunday was his birthday. I will never forget.

I bought him a joke book, his favorite pencils and a Joel Olsteen devotional book. He was grounded in church and loved my parents. They rescued him from the tragedy of my life. They protected him from any further harm due to my lifestyle. He was the baby and he was endangered by me and because of me. That breaks my soul to even write. But it's true. You see, nothing that I experienced or have shared with you in this book could possibly compare the monster I became in my own mind. I had betrayed and disappointed my own children as their mother. I got so lost in self-loathing, self-pity and negativity, that I lost sight of my job as their mom. I can never take that back or erase it. I can't fix it or change it. It was beyond my ability to repair. The credit for anything good could only go to God. No human action could simply heal or wipe away the collateral damage that ensued.

At any rate, I got in my truck and headed toward that old country church. I debated if I should go to my parent's house or the church. I finally just set my thoughts aside and turned on the radio. I tuned into the local Christian station hoping for some sort of divine connection.

To this day, I cannot tell you the name or tune of the song that began to play. I can't remember the words. The only thing I can tell you is this. It was a song that spoke to my heart and the words I do remember are "I need you." I was completely and utterly incapable of fixing any of this horrible mess. I created it for sure, but wow! God's grace surely is sufficient for every need.

I cried out. I spoke in my spirit to the Lord and begged Him for forgiveness. I sought him; I asked him for the help that I desperately needed from Him. True to His word, I asked and I received. I sought and I was found. I knocked and the door was opened to me. On that day, in that very moment in that truck, my soul was redeemed, washed, rekindled for Christ. A fire was lit and my soul was on fire.

I felt a massive burden was lifted off my shoulders. I cried the entire trip and raised my hands in praise. I knew in those moments that not only was I forgiven, but I was completely delivered and I felt different. I felt the strength of God like never before in my life. For when I was weak, He was strong. Yes, "Jesus loves me this I know for the Bible tells me so."

I decided I would go to my parents' house before going to church. I was not only on time, but early. For those who know me, they know I would not only be minutes late, but sometimes hours late. But today was my son's birthday. I wished my son a happy birthday and had planned to give him the best birthday present ever. I told no one what I had done or what I was planning to do. We got in the church and had a great service. When the pastor had the altar call, I immediately moved. You see, I had already received what God intended for me. I was forgiven—of it all. But I needed to do it publicly.

This is the incredible part. The door was opened for prayer. Lots of prayer. People who had been fervently praying for me the past five years joined with me at the altar and prayed over me. They saw their prayers answered that day. They saw the seed of prayer bring forth much fruit. They could see it in me. They knew God had done a work in me that day and this made them so relieved. They all joined me in celebrating my commitment to Christ. It was an amazing day.

We went to my parents' house afterward and Christopher enjoyed a party with the gifts. That joke book would be something that would be used in the months ahead. It was a wonderful celebration, no doubt. We even returned to church that evening for my niece's baptism. It was a great day in the Lord. Everyone was confident all would be well. They were even more convinced that I would go into court the next day, return home and begin my new journey with Christ. No one had any idea what was about to unfold in the next few hours.

You see, I didn't go to church or rededicate my life to Christ to make a deal with him. I was willing to accept whatever punishment I was given, understanding that if it wasn't in *my* favor, I would still have *God's* favor. I was ready and equipped. All of my years of walking with the Lord returned to my heart as if the pause button had been pushed to play.

REDEEMED & RESTORED: All My Hope Is in Jesus

The next morning, I went to work. My parents and I diligently worked together to make sure previous fines for other charges were taken care of before court. We had all of our ducks in a row. But my stomach was in knots. Before I left work, I organized it all in a manner that someone could come in behind me. My employer had even written a letter for me and couldn't imagine I would never return to that job.

CHAPTER 5
Path to Prison
Faithful while Fearful

I felt sick to my stomach the whole day. We all made preparations. With the exception of my youngest child, all of my children were preparing to go to court. My parents and best friend were also there to show their support. I had hired an attorney who was certainly not anything like a Harvard graduate, and the proceedings were about to begin.

I recall that on my way to court that I had given my daughter everything needed for accessing my phone and my accounts, just in case. Of course, they all thought I was overreacting and that we would go out to eat together following court. I had two cigarettes left in my pack. On the way to court and in front of the courthouse, as I smoked them, they tasted horrible. I knew in my soul that this was God delivering me of this last addiction. Actually, I think this already took place. This was simply confirmation. I knew with this, it meant I would need to be free from this addiction to do the things that were ahead of me.

Before court, my attorney took me to the side. We had a plea deal in play. It was to be recommended that I would receive time served and probation. However, that is not at all what happened.

We entered the courtroom and as the case was being heard, there were elements that had not been discussed with me ahead of time. Statements were read and testimonies were shared that were complete lies. Of course, I was guilty of contributing. However, the extreme acts that were presented as facts were nowhere near the truth. The lawyer never objected to anything. I believe the solicitor and the lawyer had already decided my fate without me. The judge stated that this was the most egregious case of contributing that he had ever heard. I would agree—if what had been presented as truth were true. However, indeed it was not.

I couldn't defend myself and the attorney didn't defend me either. I think that he felt I should go to prison and he worked with the solicitor to achieve that end. I'm not sure how a plea deal usually works, but I am fairly sure that what I pleaded to is certainly not what I got sentenced to, by any stretch of the imagination.

Once the case was presented, it was time for the judge to cast his decision and seal my fate. I recall a complete and utter feeling of shock and disbelief as the sentencing portion unfolded. I almost felt faint and recall just shutting down in my mind.

I was remanded as property of SCDC (South Carolina Department of Corrections) and given a sentence of three years, suspended to 1 year with one year of alcohol treatment in addition to three years of probation. My family was devastated and in complete shock. I was handcuffed and removed from the courtroom. That would be the last time my family would see me until my release from prison. They were shaken.

I was taken to the holding cell. I had no idea what was in store for me, but I recall the shock of it all. I questioned God and I cried in terror of the unknown. I actually laid down on the floor of the holding cell and wept. I knew was going to prison. I was a convict and I was utterly clueless about the implications of this for my life.

Once court was over, I stayed in that holding cell until it was time to be transported to the prison where I would be processed for my sentencing. The facility I would be taken to was a maximum security, Level 2 female prison in Columbia, South Carolina. Graham (Camille Griffin) Correctional Institution housed special needs women 17 years of age and older. It also functioned as a major special management unit with the ability to house female death row inmates and county safe-keepers. To look at their website, it didn't seem so bad. Living there was a completely different story.

I was shackled and handcuffed. Then, I was loaded into a transport van for the two-hour drive to my new home. I still had street clothes on and the cuffs and the shackles were painful. The seats were super small and we were packed in tightly. I filled the area more than the others due to the extra weight. This was likely the most uncomfortable situation I had been in with a group of strangers in my entire life.

PRISON TO PROSPERITY WITH PURPOSE

This van was divided into two parts. One side was for women, the other for men. We couldn't see each other, but we could hear one another. The men were saying very inappropriate things and this was the beginning of my new reality. There were no windows and we could see nothing. We sat on a hard bench that was just wide enough for us to fit in the back. Again, we were packed in tightly.

The first thing that runs through your mind is what are these other people in the van going to prison for. Some would be short sentences, like mine. Some were starting life sentences. But none of us would know exactly how long we would be in prison and how long the actual time-served would be. I believe that is part of the torture of the sentencing. From the moment you start your time, you calculate and recalculate based on other inmate speculations of when you will complete your sentence. My parents were told I would be there no more than three months. That was not at all correct.

We arrived and they unloaded us. We were all attached to one another to prevent escapes. We entered a building and the processing began. This would prove to be the most humiliating experience of my entire life. I will never forget how I felt in those moments. Not only was I in complete shock, I was entering the beginning of a mental process that only God could guide me through.

The first process I would embark upon was called the reception and evaluation (R&E) process. This was where they would receive, assess, classify and assign all inmates sentenced to 91 days or more.

PATH TO PRISON: Faithful while Fearful

Generally, it would take anywhere from 30-90 days to get your classification and begin what one would identify as "normal prison life."

I was so thankful I had God to carry me through this sentence. Without Him, I would not have made it through. Many did not make it out alive. Some even took their own lives, while would be transferred. Among the inmates, there were those who would become targets of bullying and harassment. I decided to take the stance of keeping my mouth shut and my eyes down. My superpower of invisibility was the key to my success during this process. It would help me do this time, however long it would be.

I was looking at three years. But in these moments, I could barely see myself getting through the next few hours. As we entered, we began being stripped of our humanity. First, the shoes and socks went. They were thrown in the trash.

After that, we were placed in a room that had a video playing about sexual harassment and assault on inmates by inmates and staff. It was like those old PSA videos we watched in school. This is also when I got the first taste of prison food. At times I can't recall what I had for dinner last night, but I can tell you what I had that day. It was a crusty hot dog with a pile of nasty beans and a lump of flavorless coleslaw. We were definitely not at home anymore, but of course, I ate it. I was hungry.

We were then told to strip down completely. Our clothes would either be tossed or recycled for inmates who were to be released. We were searched *completely*. Nothing was left unexamined, that's for sure. I was never one to be comfortable with my body image to start with, so this was horrible. I will skip those details for you.

I will never forget the walk to the shower. I could hardly bear the thought of this part of the process. The water was harsh and it ensured that your hair would be completely stripped of anything. It efficiently removed many of the vibrant colors some had prior to their sentence. We were given lice shampoo and directed to put it in our hair and on our bodies and then we had to stand in the shower without the water running until we were told to turn it back on. We were directed the whole way through this "prison-christening" process. It was incredibly unpleasant and completely humiliating.

Then there were the cameras. The photos they take are not meant for memoirs. They are meant to be able to identify your body should you turn up maimed or dead. They documented every tattoo and piercing. They warned you that should any others show up, you would be in violation of the huge number of rules that you were expected to understand and agree to. I think every angle was accounted for during these photoshoots. On top of that, we had to describe our tattoos.

After we completed this process, we received our uniforms and our bag of necessities. They were certainly not fancy in any way. They were super basic, to say the least. We also received a flat pillow and a mat for our beds. We would carry this large bag, the pillow and the mat to the remaining areas until we reached our assigned cell for R&E.

The next step was to get your photo and your information to create your badge ID. This must be worn at all times. It would be what was used to identify you for everything. This would be the exact moment when you become a number. Once you obtained this, you went through a short screening like if you went to the emergency room. They asked all the general questions and collected your health history and information.

If you had mental issues, more than likely you would remain at this facility. It was the lower of the only two available prisons for women in South Carolina. This prison was the one we refer to as being "run by the inmates." The CO's (correctional officers) didn't wield as much authority and inmates often got away with a lot more than at the Level 3 prison, Leath Correctional Institution.

Camille Graham was located only two hours from my family, making it was closer to home. I was hoping that I would be housed there. In all honesty, although I knew I was completely healed by God, I still listed all of my mental issues, including anxiety and depression, in the hope that I would stay at this facility. Imagine that—hoping to stay at a prison. Yes, this was now my life.

The next step in processing was medical. We would give blood samples, urine samples and be tested for everything. Some of the women had a hard time with the blood samples due to excessive scaring from intravenous drug use. Others who had Hep C would also be identified separately. Of course, there were others with illnesses like diabetes, HIV, cancer and so on. They were from all walks of life—mothers, daughters, wives, sisters, friends.

But all of that would be reduced to a number. I will never forget mine. I was no longer Malenka or Marsha or Michelle or Auntchelle or Marchelle or Honey or Babe or Sweetie or Baby Doll. Nope. I was now simply inmate #373699. That's all. I was labeled as a number and I was treated as such. I had no rights to speak of and I had no privileges. I wasn't even viewed as a human being. I was a number—nothing more.

During one of my assessments, I had the pleasure of meeting an angel sent by God. I broke down privately in her office. They weren't allowed to give us anything, but she placed a small candy bar at the edge of the desk and excused herself for a moment and made a remark that let me know it was for me without actually giving it to me.

That bite of chocolate was the best thing in the world. It was my comfort food. But more than that, it was her act of kindness that touched my soul. When she returned, she advised me to dry my tears and toughen up to get through this time. She encouraged me to take things one moment at a time and not to look at everything as being so big. She was exactly what I needed at the time, and I'm convinced that she was sent by God. She was a messenger whom He sent to me and I was blessed.

PATH TO PRISON: Faithful while Fearful

We were poked and prodded for hours. After they completed the processing and assessment portion, the next step was waiting on classification. This was a daily goal for each inmate, to get classified. Being classified meant you got just a bit more info on the time you would serve and where you would serve that time.

For the next 60 days, I would be housed with a girl who was actually from the area I lived in. I know God placed me with her, without a doubt. Being from the same area was a good icebreaker when it came to introductions.

As I was being escorted to meet my future roommate, the gravity of it all was sinking in. This section of the prison was self-contained and it housed everyone who was waiting to be classified. It was a rectangle with a top and bottom row. Youthful offenders were held separately, but no one else was classified according to their cellmate, with exception of gangs.

The inmate-to-correctional officer ratio was about 10:1—which to me didn't seem like very good odds. I was well aware of the danger that I could potentially face on a regular basis. I was housed with people with charges ranging from shoplifting to cooking dope to murder. We were all housed together.

I was given my cell number and guided through this massive rectangle of confusion. Of course, my cell was on the upper level and I was terrified. As I was taken to my cell, I began to see what my near future was to become. The cell was no bigger than about 6'x8'. The door had a flap through which they would pass necessary things. As you opened the door, there was an open steel toilet with a sink attached to it on the left side of the cell. Right next to that was a one-piece desk/stool combo and the metal bunk bed butted up to that.

This cell was equipped for only two people. However, there is a great deal of overcrowding in prisons and several cells had an extra cot to house three inmates. I was so thankful that was not my situation. In addition, I had a decent cellmate sent by God, and I would keep her during my entire time in R&E. Not many were fortunate enough to have this happen to them.

I had my sheet and a very thin blanket. I was required to make my bed a certain way, and did so. There was no canteen, no books, no excess of anything. It was very basic. You had your assigned roll of toilet paper, a small bottle of shampoo, soap, washcloths, towels, uniforms, toothpaste and toothbrush. That was it. All I wanted was a Bible and a pen. Let me be clear: those were not things we had access to right away. As a matter of fact, we were limited to a pencil, when I finally did get one.

From the moment you arrive, you begin the prison math game. It's really the absolute worst part of doing your time. It becomes an obsession. You see, you are given a maximum "out-date," but you know that based on some sort of percentages you actually won't serve all of your time. This number is based on a variety of things.

Some jobs on the inside reduce additional time off from your sentence, so everyone would want those right off the bat. Educational classes and special programs were also a way to get time shaved off. Lastly, there were a variety of programs that could potentially score you a reduction as well.

But before any of that, you had to be classified. That was the first goal. This was time that would drag on slower than you ever thought possible. You see, time in prison moves at a *much* slower pace. There is no busyness. It is literally just time. You count every second and try your best to find things to fill each one.

During this first part, there is very little to do. You begin with getting to know your cellmate and pray that you have at least something in common and that they are not the worst thing you could imagine. There are seriously a lot of things that could be a potential issue in such close quarters. I mean, let's be honest, you are sharing a toilet that has no privacy.

They fill you in on what they have learned since being placed there and give you all the info they have received up to that point. They are the expert for you. The next task is to figure out the schedule: showers, meals and what you are able to do while waiting.

There was a small bookshelf at the end of the hall. One for the top floor cells and one for the bottom. This would be the target. In this tiny library are books that each have their own set of issues. Missing pages, missing series, missing covers. Honestly, it didn't matter because reading was something to do.

PRISON TO PROSPERITY WITH PURPOSE

I personally just wanted to get my hands on a Bible. Little did I know these would be similar to a basic Dollar Tree Bible, at best. That was my first order of business. This miniature library would house only a few items. Among them were Bibles, some sci-fi books and a few biographies.

I found two worthy reads for myself. The first that struck me was *Karla Faye Tucker Set Free: Life and Faith on Death Row* by Linda Strom and *Limitless Life* by Derwin L. Gray. They were small books, so I only read a little bit each day. I made sure to savor them slowly and not get in a big rush to complete them. I took my time.

The other commodity that I wanted was pen and paper. I was fortunate enough to manage to get five sheets of copy paper and a pencil. (Pens weren't allowed due to inmates using them to tattoo one another.) I would use all of these books and take notes, as I read. I wrote as small as I could on the unlined paper, as to not waste any space. You see, I knew once it was used, it was gone and I wouldn't have access to more. The feelings of scarcity began to set in and I became a collector of sorts. Why? Because everything I owned was gone. Nothing I had was mine any longer and it all belonged to the state.

The next thing was figuring out when I would be able to call my family. Up to this point, it had been the longest day of my entire life, and it was still not over. I found out the phone schedule, how to get funds on your books, and other things. Absolutely nothing was easy. Nothing. Period!

PATH TO PRISON: Faithful while Fearful

The one thing that I did have plenty of was time. Most of this time would be spent trying to figure things out and just occupy my mind with anything. I thought a lot. I even thought about how I could pass the time in a way that it didn't seem so long. I prayed and asked God to show me His purpose. I knew there was a plan—I just couldn't see it yet. I asked for His favor and protection. I had no idea how I would get through the coming days. The only thing I knew was that God was right there with me and would not leave me.

I won't go into all the details that I experienced during this time, but I will say that I was happier than ever once I got my classification and could move forward in completing my time in prison. You were prepared in anticipation that once this happened, you would have more information to understand when you would actually be released. I had no idea of my release date until only a couple of days before I left. That was very difficult to manage, to say the least.

Finally, moving day had arrived and I was classified. I was told only to pack up what I needed and that I was being shipped to the other prison. Although this was the step I had been waiting for, I was immediately filled with fear. As I mentioned earlier, this was a maximum-security Level 3 prison. It was a complete controlled-movement facility and you had very few privileges. It was not something I was looking forward to at all.

We all got handcuffed and shackled and were transported with the small amount of belongings we had accumulated. The ride on the bus was about two hours, and not pleasant at all. We did get to see the outside, which was really nice. And, it was a bit odd after two months to be in a vehicle again. You wouldn't think you would miss something like that, but you do.

We arrived with our bags and began to be processed in what would be my new home until I would be released. It was similar to when we were processed into R&E, but a little less rigid, or so it seemed.

I was assigned a cell and a bed. I was so relieved to find out that I did not get assigned to the top bunk again. That was a bit easier in R&E because I could get up into bed using the table. But the Lord really watched out for me in this instance. I was pretty heavy and I don't think I would have been able to get on the top bunk.

The prison layout had blocks for inmates. Each block was kind of like a neighborhood and they were named. It was really odd that each took on neighborhood characteristics. Inside each building, there were four pods with two levels in each. Each pod is where the cells were located. Each cell would be assigned three inmates due to overcrowding.

These cells were slightly larger. They had a locker and a small desk. Living in close quarters with two people under these conditions was a challenge. But now, there would be three of us sharing a cell. I would have several cellmates shuffled throughout my short stay there. Some have since gone home to their families.

I quickly learned that inside prison, there was also "jail." On the street, you would know it as "isolation." But it's not exactly how you would picture it at all. It was the same type of building, but they were more severe in restricting privileges like food and warmth. I was fortunate enough not to end up in isolation. Some of my cellmates would not be so lucky.

One got in a fight and the other was caught having sex with another inmate. You could end up in jail simply for not being ready when count was called. Count time would happen multiple times a day and you would have to be in your designated space and say your inmate number. That is how I ended up memorizing it, of course. Needless to say, I would never forget it—373699.

As I reflect on those I lived with during that time, it makes me sad to know what happened to them later. One, who was released, was headed back in before I had completed my time. Another, who was released after me, ended up murdered. Others, I have seen ebb and flow. I have kept in touch with some via Facebook. There is one woman I have stayed connected with who is still in the place that I was able to put behind me.

This amazing woman is my friend Jenn. She was sentenced to 18 years. Of the 18, she has done 10 already. We stay in touch and I pray with her and send her money from time to time to encourage her during the remainder of her time. I'm constantly checking the new prison reform bill hoping for her early release.

It sounds like she did a really horrible thing, right? In our state, you don't actually have to be the perpetrator of the crime. But, she was caught under the law that states, "the hand of one is the hand of all." All you have to do is to be in the wrong place, at the wrong time, with the wrong person. She fully complied and assisted law enforcement in the investigation and was cooperative. Yet, she still got a heavy sentence and that wasn't even considered.

Prison reform is desperately needed. There are many who, without a doubt, do belong in prison. Sure, most of them have broken the law. But to be punished on the level of some whom I got to know really broke my heart. I pray the early release bill is passed soon and I would ask you to pray as well. There are many who are incarcerated who aren't monsters. I was one of them.

It's because of this experience that when I see a post on Facebook of how people in prison get three squares a day and all of these amazing benefits, it full-on enrages me. Those people are sadly misinformed. As a matter of fact, there were many times that it was only two-a-day. Without canteen privileges, which were pretty expensive, you didn't get a whole lot of food. Moreover, the food you did get lacked a desirable flare, to say the least. Please, don't ever post foolish things like that on Facebook. If you have not been to prison, you honestly have no right to cast judgment or have an opinion on that matter.

Okay, rant over...

On to the next phase of my incarceration: We settled in and did our time together. Most of the time I was there, we only left the pod for meals, when we were not on lockdown and church.

You would think, reading the website, there were all kinds of programs. However, that would not apply to me, a short-timer. Those are reserved for people somewhere in the middle. People like me had a difficult time because no one wants to connect with you. They treat you differently. You are considered a nuisance. On top of that, I voiced my faith, which wasn't the most popular stance and I wasn't winning any popularity contests.

I spent my time in the Word, studying. After a few months, I was able to get a small radio that enabled me to listen to the one Christian station I could get reception on and watch TV on the occasional Sunday morning. But church—that was not easy at all. It certainly is not what you would compare to church on the outside.

In the free world, you can worship in a variety of ways and it isn't hindered by the authorities. In prison, you are still a convict and you don't have the freedom to move as the Spirit moves you, so to speak. It's very limited. Outside preachers would come in to share the Word. And, although they were usually really good, corporate prayer was difficult, at best. It was less than a desirable church experience.

Also, there were many who went for the wrong reasons, and there were only a select few who could go. I finally got to the point that I just wouldn't go. Near the end, I stayed in my cell most of the time. Well, I actually got punished for the last 30 days to be confined to my cell majority of the time.

PRISON TO PROSPERITY WITH PURPOSE

You see, there are evil people in there, no doubt. There was one girl, a "lifer," who had it out for me. She didn't like me and she didn't want me to go home—so she set me up. She gave me a box and asked me to write someone's name on it—which was against the rules. I did it and I got caught. I ended up doing the last portion of my time isolated from the rest in my cell.

I lost canteen privileges as well, and it was at that time when I got to know Jenn. I could purchase things that were considered necessities—shirts, shoes, etc.—just not food. As a result, I engaged in what is referred to as "traffic and trading"—I took the risk. She bought food and traded me for the toiletries and other things that I bought for her. Food is really the only thing you have in there. I was fortunate that I had funds for it. I needed comfort food then more than ever.

I really didn't get to know Jenn until I was released. We are really close now and I am honored to be her friend. I think of her often. When things go on in our world, it has a different effect on those inside. Right now, I'm concerned for her with the current coronavirus pandemic. More than likely they will be placed on lockdown. Lockdown is the worst thing of all.

When you're on lockdown, you don't go to church. You don't go outside. You don't go to the cafeteria. You don't leave your cell. You don't freely go to the bathroom. You have to shower in order. You don't get phone calls. You don't get TV. You don't get to use the kiosk for emails. You just cannot fathom that until you are in

PATH TO PRISON: Faithful while Fearful

that position. It is truly difficult to only have your mind to keep you busy. Therefore, it was important that I use lockdown wisely. It was during those times that my Bible provided so much strength for me. I don't know what I would have done without it.

Growing up, I wasn't much of a reader. I'm still not a big reader. But in prison, you read—*a lot*. God used that time to prepare me for what He had in store for me. He strengthened me not just for being in prison, but for when I would be released. He filled my heart, my mind and my soul with His Word and that is never in vain.

As I look back, my time in prison was laying the foundation for my eventual future success. Without having the time to commit to immerse myself in the living Word of God, I would never have been able to live out that complete deliverance. God certainly worked *all* things for my good and for His glory.

As time passed, I was able to collect a few books and devotions. This was great for me. I loved the small library that I was able to build. Other inmates noticed and they began to come to me for spiritual counsel and prayer. They knew I was spiritually grounded and were willing to share. Let me tell you, the devil did not like this one bit. He would send those whom he could control against me in many ways. It got so bad at one point that I almost intentionally did not stand for count in order to get moved into isolation.

You see, bullying happens and nothing is done about it. If you wanted to escape it, you would break a big enough rule to go to "jail." The easiest one to break would be to sit during count. I was so close to doing it. Fortunately, in the end, I decided to persevere through it and pray. No one could help me, except my God and I had to trust that His ability was not limited by prison.

I could write an entire book on my prison experiences, but that isn't what I really have on my heart to share with this book. You see, the purpose of this book is to tell you enough for you to truly comprehend how good the God is whom I serve. That, no matter what, He has been there for me. No matter what, He has provided for me. I have learned that if we submit ourselves to Him and walk obediently in what He asks of us, He will bless us—*and do so abundantly.*

This is my story of how God took me from finding my way at the bottom, in prison—broken and alone—to a place of healing and prosperity. I serve a mighty God who has done more for me in my life than I could ever do for myself or even imagine. I pray that as you finish this book, you will be moved. I pray that you will be moved to action. I pray that will be inspired and encouraged.

I have heard my mentor, Jessie Lee Ward, as well as Les Brown (a motivational speaker) both make a statement that I've adopted. I say this not to impress you, but to impress *upon* you that if God will do it for me, He will do it for you—but we must do our part.

God took me from a place of darkness and imprisonment to the place of a prosperous life. I share these things, not to be boastful, but to be a testimony of what is possible with God. God doesn't have limitations. But sometimes we limit what we allow Him to do in our lives.

CHAPTER 6

Restoration & the Road to Prosperity

Life, Take-Two Begins

On March 1, 2017, I was released from Leath Correctional Institution into the custody of my best friend, Vicki. She drove four hours to come and pick me up. Without this amazing friend, I would never have been able to get through my time in prison. She managed and sent my money. She took my calls. She wrote to me. She loved me. She was a rock for me to lean on during that time in my life. I am forever grateful for her and what she did—and she will never know the full extent of the love I have for her.

On this day, I discovered, my journey had just begun. I was incarcerated for a total of 192 days. I didn't see my family or friends during that entire time. I will say that husband number 3 came to visit me once, and that meant the world to me. Also, while I was in prison, I missed the birth of my first granddaughter, Layla. I'm forever grateful for the wife of my children's father. She sent me the only Christmas card I received while in prison and the first photos of my Layla Payla. I tear up just reflecting on the moment I received those in the mail.

For me, that was the worst part of my time. I can't ever change the fact that I wasn't there the day she was born. Just that thought still makes me very sad. It hurts me far into the depths of my soul—to the point that I cannot bear to even see photos of her as a baby. It's just too painful for me and a reminder that I wasn't there to enjoy her first months. She was already four months old when I was released.

In the coming months, I would have another granddaughter and I was also unable to be a part of her life until she was six months old. You see, this was all fallout from the lifestyle I had lived. They are natural consequences I had to face. God does not just suddenly pour out rainbows and unicorns on your life because you decide to submit. You still have to work through the clean-up phase of life. However, rest assured, He will never leave your side. That is important to remember and is a very critical part of this story.

Don't ever think that God owes you a thing. He doesn't. Every good and perfect gift comes from Him. But He is certainly not required to pour out abundance on you. The Word is really clear on how you receive blessings in life. It's pretty simple: Obedience. In order to be obedient, you must be submitted. In order to be submitted, you must be humble. God will not bless those who are

RESTORATION AND THE ROAD TO PROSPERITY
Life, Take-Two Begins

proud and full of themselves. That is something that I must always stay mindful of in my success. It's also why I remind you that I don't share any of this to impress you. Again, I share it to impress *upon* you that God can bless you too. He is waiting on you.

This is the chapter. This is the one that I must get right. I have been trained to start strong and finish strong. The stuff in the middle may soon be forgotten, but the way you begin and the way you end will be remembered over anything else. It's my honor and privilege to write this book—and I pray that as you have read it, you have been inspired, encouraged, and ignited into action.

Let's be honest: You've read this far to find out what happened after prison. What created a shift in my life that resulted in success, abundance, and prosperity? What's the secret? There is no secret, really. But I will share with you the events that unfolded and the actions I took to arrive at this place that I have found.

There are two words that I feel need to be stressed and kept in the forefront of your minds as you read this chapter. One is gratitude and the other is contentment. You see, I have had much and I have had little. However, in all situations, regardless of how great or small, the one thing I know for certain is these two elements are a must have and are non-negotiable. I would say that these two attributes, especially in our world today, are scarce and largely unpracticed. I would encourage you to embrace and practice both gratitude and contentment in your journey if you want to find true prosperity.

You see, I was prosperous before I was released. The moment of prosperity came in a moment of humility. As soon as I asked for Jesus to take the reins, it all changed. Were there difficulties, tears, challenge, and desperate times? Of course. But through each one, I found opportunity to trust in Jesus and His promises in the Word to bring me through it all. They were simply steppingstones to prepare me for what was ahead. The cycle of learning will never cease. It's an integral part of walking with Christ.

Let's start with my release date. When I arrived home, my family was so happy to see me. I met my granddaughter for the first time and held her. Although my heart was touched, if I am completely honest, there was a disconnect of emotion that I did not expect. She was a stranger. We had to get to know each other. I missed out on her first four months and we started at square one.

That brings me to the whole family. That is where we were all starting. They were on pins and needles. They desperately wanted to believe that I had been redeemed and converted. But they had that hesitation and fear that what I had may be what others referred to as "prison religion." You see, there are many who find Jesus within the walls of prison. But when they get released, they fall right back into their old ways.

There was nothing I could say or do to convince them. This was something only time would reveal. I had created a space of broken trust and disappointment. But with the help of the Holy Spirit to guide me, I was able to overcome that stigma.

RESTORATION AND THE ROAD TO PROSPERITY
Life, Take-Two Begins

My parents set me and my middle son up in a very small but comfortable camper. It was actually perfect because it was not too large. One of the things to which I had adapted was a quiet setting and small spaces. You would actually be surprised at how loud the world is once you've been in prison. Just going to Walmart could be overwhelming. I had to reintegrate back into society and this was a good start.

Not everyone can live in such small spaces though, I will admit. And, my son had some adjusting to do. We got along well for the most part. But the doubt planted in the back of his mind made him wonder. At one point, we ended up in a huge argument and he left home. I believe he thought I would return to the old me. To his surprise, as well as to everyone else's, I did not. He ended up returning back to the camper with me and we patched things up after a few weeks.

As I stated before, my second granddaughter was born just a few months later. I wasn't allowed to be a part of that experience. My daughter still harbored a great deal of resentment toward me and was completely unconvinced of the change that had taken place. The whole family tried to tell her how different I was, but to no avail. She wasn't buying it and she kept me at a distance. There were some difficulties during birth, but we ended up with a healthy little baby, Ava. We now call her by the nickname, Babers. Her Uncle Matt Matt gave her that special name.

My daughter lived in Tennessee and I wasn't able to see or visit her. I was on probation for the next year and a half, providing I kept all of the expectations, and acquired all the needed travel passes. Eventually, she did begin to speak to me and I was able to go visit. When my daughter saw me, she couldn't deny the change. We spent several days together at a cute little AirBNB. It was amazing. Again, the immediate connection was not there, but it would grow in time.

We did the best we could through the distance. I knew she was in a bad spot in her life as well. She had been on drugs and an alcoholic and ended up being with someone who was mentally and physically abusive. When she got pregnant with Ava, she left all of that behind. Unfortunately, he did not. While I could not change her circumstances, I could pray.

Back to my release in March: I had my camper and I attended my local church as much as possible. I began to become active in my community as well. But I was tired. I was out of shape. I was struggling physically. You see, living in prison not only packed on the pounds, it increased my desire for massive amounts of carbs. This was where a lot of work that would need to be done.

I jumped on the keto craze. I saw others who had results, and I was desperate to have some for myself. Coming from confinement, I was so out of shape that even going for a walk was a huge task. So, I started doing research.

During all of this, I was blessed enough to reconnect with a

RESTORATION AND THE ROAD TO PROSPERITY
Life, Take-Two Begins

friend from the past who was willing to give me some work handling his bookkeeping again. I recognized that this was also a blessing from God and I took it. I knew this was my start. No one else would hire me, being an ex-con. I mean, let's be realistic here—I now had a record. I wasn't willing to lie about it either. I was very upfront with everyone and I was confident that the Lord would provide. I mean, I had no bills to worry about, so any income was helpful.

As I began to get income, I tithed. Let me explain what a tithe actually is, for me. You see, most people instantly think about money. Ten percent can be pretty tough to let go of in difficult times, no doubt. However, for me, it was also tithing my time. If God blesses you, you need to be faithful. If you do not give back to God, how can you expect Him to continue to bless you? This is obedience. I would say that no matter what you have, recognize it is *all* from God. You simply cannot out-give God. He blesses us to the level that we allow Him to bless us. I believe that it's all based on trust. Do we really trust that God will provide? There have been times it was really hard to trust. But I assure you that if you follow what God puts in your heart, you simply cannot go wrong.

There I was—on probation, on food stamps, living in a camper. Yet, my heart was full of gratitude. I was blessed. I was free. I was in awe. This was the first time in my life that I had lived with so little, yet been so grateful. I could now truly recognize the truest meaning of freedom. Looking back, I had more freedom in prison than most people have in their day-to-day lives.

Things were progressing and I was looking for the next area of opportunity to create a better life for myself and my family. My parents were in very poor health and my children began following in our footsteps with food addiction. Therefore, when I discovered keto, I began to recruit them all and introduce them to what I was doing.

For the first month, I drank cup after cup of what's called "bulletproof coffee." And I tried a variety of products that were supposed to aid in success. I was watching videos and doing tons of research. After an entire month, I lost zero pounds and I felt like a failure.

How is it that God could deliver me from a life of drug addiction, alcoholism, being in prison, but I still battled with my weight so much? I was at my wits' end. I was looking for a solution. I prayed about it. God's Word teaches us that we have not because we ask not—and so, yeah, I asked.

He answered me in ways greater than I could have ever dreamed. In my research efforts, I stumbled upon this curly haired woman who was cooking in her kitchen. Oddly enough, she's not someone I normally would have been drawn to either. Let's be honest here— she was vegan, and I most certainly was not.

However, there was something attractive about her that I felt drawn to as I watched. She made one statement that jumped out at me. She said, "If you want to know how I cook dinner for my family

RESTORATION AND THE ROAD TO PROSPERITY
Life, Take-Two Begins

and make a living from home, message me." Just like that, she went back to cooking her vegan dish.

I'm convinced that the Lord wanted me to be watching that video and hear exactly what I needed to hear on that day. It spoke to me. But I had been duped so many times in the past—and you know what I mean. Those pills, scams, diets and all the things that had never lived up to the hype—the old bait and switch. But I believe God sent me to this exact space.

I decided to connect with this woman and began a journey that ultimate changed the trajectory of my entire life. I asked her how she made money. Was it a sponsor? She said, "Kind of ..." She began to explain this amazing product that I had no idea even existed.

In conversation, she offered what had provided such success for her financially and physically. She wasn't pushy and she certainly didn't try to "sell" me on this product in any way. I thought, "Wait. There must be a catch. She is gonna try to sell me." But she never did. She just let me navigate through where I was to get to the point of convincing myself that this was a good investment.

Let me tell you, the investment was significant. I had to sacrifice to scrape together just the cost of a trial. I finally had enough to check it out for ten days. I told her that it had better work—and taste good. But if it did, I would be all in.

When I got the package, my heart dropped and I immediately

thought, "What have I done? Scammed again? Lord, please let this work." I needed help. But I did know that all of the hope I ever had or would have was found in Jesus. So, I jumped right in. I ripped open the first sachet, mixed it in some water and drank it.

At first, I honestly thought, okay, she said I would have better energy, better focus, better mood, better mental clarity and better sleep. I think it's just in my head. But we'll see tomorrow. Obviously, I had some major trust issues. But hey, who wouldn't? Nothing I had ever tried that promised a better life, outside of Christ, actually worked for me.

Day 2: I did the same thing. I wasn't particularly fond of this flavor, but I wasn't gonna let it go to waste at the price I paid for it. So, I drank it. What do you know? It happened again. I felt those things she had told me I would feel. At that moment, I said to myself, "Self, if we feel this way again tomorrow, this has to be legit." I prayed for this, so why was I surprised?

Of course, day 3 was no different. I was shaken. This could not be working like they promised. I mean, it had to be a complete Godsend—and that's exactly what it was, without a doubt. I said to myself, "Self, if we feel this way again tomorrow, we are spending every dime we have to get onboard. We *must* tell the world about this product."

Sure enough, as you can expect at this point, day 4 was a hit. I immediately messaged this woman who would not only become a mentor, but a friend, and told her I wanted all in. I waited on my

RESTORATION AND THE ROAD TO PROSPERITY
Life, Take-Two Begins

pay for the month and used every cent of a month's pay and invested in myself and my future. I had zero clue as to where it would take me.

As soon as the product arrived, I quickly began to post photos of it to "sell" this amazing product. Did that sound *at all* like how I discovered it? *Nope.* But, I was like a wild stallion that couldn't be broken or trained. I was super-excited and managed to convince my mom and my best friend to join me in this journey. It was working for all of us. We did have a few underlying conditions that slowed our progress, but we were determined.

My mentor was full of patience. Although I refused to do what she tried to show me, she hung in there and continued to patiently guide me when I would express my frustration in my unsuccessful attempts at sales. I thank God for her because if she did not stay the course and allow me to come to her, I would have never made it this far. If you have someone in your organization who is that wild card, persevere! It could prove to be the one who radically changes the world.

At any rate, over the course of the next few months, I would attend events. I would participate in training sessions. I would become more and more coachable. Once I used the systems that were there all along, they began to be fruitful. You know, this is so much like God. When I reflect on this, I believe He used this business in so many ways to nurture my walk with Him. You see, we must be teachable in order to be blessed. We must be obedient. If we aren't, then we'll keep getting rerouted, as this mentor did for me, until we get it.

There were many spiritual awakenings along the way in this journey. I had much to learn. I had to learn tolerance, patience, consistency and persistence. I had to learn that not everyone will like me. I had to learn that no matter what I see, God will open doors, if I only walk in humility and obedience.

It was not long before things began to shift. I was drinking the product for free and making a decent income. I had more than doubled my monthly income. Today, I am in awe at the shift in my income. Never in a million years did I imagine I could make any kind of real money. I mean, honestly, I thought $75,000 a year was rich-man status. On top of that, I never thought I would reach that kind of income. I just could not envision it.

As I began to make progress with some success, I introduced my whole family to it. This kit I got, I used to share with all of them. I even shipped some to my daughter up in Tennessee. I wanted so much for her to experience a better life. I could see in her eyes the struggles she was having as a new mom in an environment that would tear her down spiritually, financially, mentally, emotionally and physically.

I got the call I knew was coming soon. She was in tears. She had enough. She was ready to come home. The best part was that God

RESTORATION AND THE ROAD TO PROSPERITY
Life, Take-Two Begins

already knew all of this and had prepared us. I talked to my parents and we all agreed she needed to come home—so as our family does, we rallied to help. My middle son, who lived with me, had the cash on hand and I had money coming in that I could pay him back for it. We merged our resources and had her and my granddaughter on a flight that same day. They were coming home.

I was overjoyed. Yes, overjoyed. We were all going to live in this tiny camper together with one bed and a couch, but we were family, and families sacrifice. We could not wait to see and help with that precious baby girl. She was six months old by this time. My daughter was just not prepared for the world in any way.

You see, because of the domestic abuse, she had stayed in the room with the baby most of the time. They were as sheltered as I was in prison. It broke my heart. It has taken months for these two to evolve to the confident and outgoing people they have become. And I could not be more proud. I'm in awe at the progress they've made. Moreover, my daughter came into the business as well and is experiencing the same success I did when I began.

Most of my family and friends have been recruited by me into this phenomenal company. If you want more details on that, you will need to contact me via email at prisontoprosperity@gmail.com. After all, I don't "sell" anything. I am simply living the life I was blessed with and willing to share the tools I used to do it. Make sure you put in the subject heading P2P so I know you read the book.

So here we were, three adults and a baby who was not used to being around people, living in this tiny camper. Oh, did I mention in the midst of all of this that I was cooking for my family on Facebook Live to share the keto lifestyle? That immediately became a challenge in this setting. Let me put this in perspective, this camper had less than 200 square feet. Although we loved each other, this could not last for very long.

We all lived there at no charge. My parents put us up. I only paid for the utilities. It didn't take long at all to outgrow this living arrangement. They finally offered to let me move into another camper that had much more room. But there was a catch. I had to move my youngest son in with me. He had still been living with them from before I went to prison.

I was scared, but I knew I was ready—and we did it. We let my son and daughter and granddaughter stay in the smaller camper and we moved into the "deluxe model." We even found a mini piano that fit in it perfectly.

We're very passionate about our music. The piano is how my youngest survived my time in prison. His talent is a direct result of the Holy Spirit filling his fingers and his soul with music from that time with the piano. He would play for hours on end.

This move took a bit more adjustment, but we did it. We were not in there long before things began to develop even more. We were charging ahead to a leadership spot and thriving in our finances. It

RESTORATION AND THE ROAD TO PROSPERITY
Life, Take-Two Begins

was in that camper that the Lord helped me to unlock the level in my business that would position me to earn a free car. As a result, I now drive a free Cadillac Escalade Platinum Edition. Well, let me correct that: it's $1 a month. What a blessing it is to share that with you. I mean, how else could this happen to me without God?

As the time approached for me to select my car, my parents came to me and said, "You know a luxury car doesn't really match that camper. We have a proposition." They told me they would allow me to rent the apartment connected to them. This was a big deal. First, it took a lot of faith and trust for them to offer it to me. But second, it would require me to pay rent, since it was a rental unit they had for income.

It was $200 a week. I wasn't sure I could handle that at this point. But God was completely sure. We moved in immediately and I have never struggled once with coming up with rent money. I know God has opened so many doors for me in this process.

During this time, I also was able to afford more events. I was asked to speak at one of the events on belief. Can you believe *that*? I was honored and had no idea where this might take me. I was asked to speak in front of almost 1,000 business owners working this same business on a topic I knew inside and out. Working this business has prepared me for every single thing that I am doing right now, and I know it is equipping me for what is ahead.

The moment I stepped on stage I knew what my first note would be. I started with, "I was asked to speak to you guys on belief. Anyone who knows me, knows my strongest belief is in God." That was very hard to do, believe me. But it was in that moment that I had locked in the attentions of everyone in the room. The response was amazing.

To this day, I can't recall everything that I shared on that stage. But I can tell you how I felt. I felt *empowered*. I felt God leading every single word. I had found my passion, my calling, my purpose. I knew that speaking to others about belief would be something that I would do more of in the future and I was right.

Everyone who was there was engaged. They listened to every word I had to say. They got value out of something that just was a fact in my life. They all listened intently as I shared my story.

We all have a story to tell. I believe that if we step up in obedience and share what God has done in our lives, then He can give us more to share. God is not finished with me yet, by any means. He has only just begun. But I know what I'm called to do. I know what my purpose is in life. I am filled with the passion to share it with the world.

Being on stage was just as natural and normal for me as it could possibly be. This is where my sights are set. This is why I was born. Everything I have gone through has brought me to this place. I fully intend to share the hope for a future that God can provide to you if you're open to His direction.

RESTORATION AND THE ROAD TO PROSPERITY
Life, Take-Two Begins

Where He leads, I will follow. I don't know what comes next. I'm not even quite sure how to end this book. You see, my life was prosperous before the money. I found peace, contentment, satisfaction, joy and all the things, well before money was abundant. I believe the Word to be true and God to be faithful in all things.

There are two things that I live by, and both are found in Scripture.

Matthew 6:33 *"But seek first his kingdom and his righteousness, and all these things will be added unto you."*

Proverbs 23:7 *"for as he thinks within himself, so he is…"*

The first is what I needed to make my daily motto. The second one came in time. You see, as you gain more and more control over your own thoughts, you can direct the path of your future. I don't believe you can think yourself into becoming rich. But I believe you can think yourself into becoming faithful. Being rich is just a monetary reward for making good financial decisions. Being *faithful* in an eternal reward that can benefit you in every single area of your life. *That* is the true meaning of prosperity.

I pray that you were blessed as I shared this story of hope with you. I pray that you understand, as God has led me to my mentor who shared this journey with me, He has led you to me. He brought you through the reading of this book and He has spoken to you today.

What is it that He is calling you to do? What is He taking you through? Molding you for? What is your purpose? What are you passionate about? What talents, skills and abilities did He bless you with in your life?

Jesus is calling you to something right now. What thoughts came to mind? How was your spirit moved? Do you hear the still small voice of God? *That* is what you are seeking. As the Bible teaches us, seek and you shall find.

There is a song that I hold near and dear and it is simple. "All My Hope is in Jesus." I'm thankful for everything He has brought me to and through and I pray that I will serve Him well throughout my life. I pray that as He blesses me, I am able to bless others. I pray to hear those words, "Well done, my good and faithful servant."

Sounds easy enough, right? Maybe you still are struggling with answering some of these questions for yourself. Maybe you still don't understand your purpose, your calling, your gifts. It's my prayer that as you finish reading this book that you will become enlightened and be open to a world you never even knew existed for you.

CHAPTER 7
Living on Purpose
Finding Your Purpose & Passion

I never felt like my life had purpose. I mean, that's always the toughest question, isn't it? What are your spiritual gifts, talents and natural God-given abilities? I was clueless. This lack of vision also created a serious problem with unbelief. I would suggest that vision starts and fuels your belief.

Those who know me know that I have an exceptional gift of belief. First and foremost, I have my belief in God. I'm also the person that will share my belief with others when they are lacking in belief themselves.

You see, I am a huge advocate for living in the promises of God's Word. He teaches us in Proverbs 23:7, "For as he thinks within himself, so he is…" This was something I could not implement, much less grasp for my life. I had heard about "mindset." I had tried self-help books. I would try to "speak things into existence." But my life was just bad.

At one point, the assistant manager at one of my jobs, looked at me and said, "I got nothing." I thought of myself as just being so deep into a life of failure. Everything I put effort into would crumble. It was depressing. I wanted what other people had in their lives. Why not me?

That is the exact question we all need to ask of ourselves. Read this out loud right now. "Why not me?" Try it on for size. Can you truly think of a reason why God would not want to bless you? Do you believe your purpose is hidden from you? I know I sure felt that it was beyond just a little vague to me.

So how did I find my purpose? How am I living my life with such vigor, joy, happiness and passion? How did this happen? I asked all the same questions in my search for purpose. But you don't find your purpose. You are born with it.

Psalm 139:14 says, "I will give thanks to You, for I am fearfully and wonderfully made; Wonderful are Your works, And my soul knows it very well." This scripture is the key to your purpose.

First, we need to give thanks to God. We should appreciate that He took the time to fashion us exactly as we are. Not one detail was forgotten. He assigned our strengths and understood each of the flaws that we would develop in our lives. He fearfully and wonderfully made us. He designed us with a purpose in mind just for us. He made me unique, and so are you.

That is a tough concept to grasp for most of us. You can Google

LIVING ON PURPOSE: Finding Your Purpose & Passion

it in an attempt to find out how to tap into your purpose. But I will tell you, all of the books in the world will never be able to adequately lead you in your God-given purpose that He created *only you* to fulfill.

Looking back over the years, I can clearly see my purpose existed all along. I was the person others would go to when they needed a friend or a shoulder to cry on. I was their source of borrowed belief. I was an encourager and would gladly fill their cup to the brim. I would speak words of edification into their lives. I never understood how powerful my gifts were and how God would be able to use them. Even the guidance counselor had dismissed me as a useless member of society.

What we often fail to realize is that our lack of confidence in who we are and who we were born to become is one thing that can hinders us. It's what prevents us from living out our purpose. Most times, our callings and gifts are so simple that we overlook them and take them for granted. Instead, we should be celebrating, discovering and embracing the qualities that only we can share with others. These are the things that we don't even question. They're natural to us. It's like saying to yourself, "What's so special about my hand? It belongs there." Perhaps it's part of you that you can't even see that is worlds above the rest of society.

Maybe it's cooking. Maybe it's sending mail or cards. Maybe it's editing. Maybe it's singing or playing an instrument. There are thousands upon thousands of untapped gifts in this world. Too often, people simply don't live up to their full potential because they don't realize that God is not stingy. He is a God of abundance. He is a God of plenty. He is a God who wants to fill our cup and then some.

I always had such a limited belief in what God wanted to do for me in my life. There is that Scripture again, "As a man thinks…" It wasn't until recent years that I shifted my view of who God is. I have now connected on a much more personal level with my Redeemer. My Father. My Friend. My Savior. I have grown in a much deeper relationship with Him.

You see, that distance relationship made me believe that He couldn't love me. I felt unloved for so much of my life, with the exception of my parents, of course. How could God love me so much? I now realize that it's because I am His child. I am His creation. I am His ambassador.

I regret all the years I wandered in the wilderness like the Israelites. But I can't change those things. I can only learn from them. And, I can also share my story of hope with others who feel the same way I did. I want you to know that you have a purpose. God did not just create you on accident. He created you on purpose, for a purpose. Yes, you have a purpose and it is right in front of you—and perhaps it's hiding in plain sight.

While I was in prison, I read a lot. I read more than I had ever read in my entire life. Moreover, I read the Bible and it allowed me to use my time in prison to become that ambassador for Christ. I was being prepared for this moment in time. I was being taught and filled with wisdom, knowledge and understanding. I prayed for these things daily. God answered those prayers in abundance.

When I was released, God had taken 192 days to equip me for everything that was ahead, even writing these words in this book right now. I believe with all that I am that I was meant to live my experiences and share them with you right now in this moment of time. Perhaps He is speaking to you through me right now. He wants *you* to know that He fearfully and wonderfully made you on purpose—for a purpose. Are you listening?

Nothing else fill the space that God created inside you to be filled by Him and His calling for you. It is a God-shaped space. Drugs, alcohol, relationships, people, sex, money, things, jobs, food, success or fame will never be able to fill that space. Those are all distractions to keep you from living in your purpose.

God made me aware of these things during the intimate times we spent together. I'm talking hours upon hours of reading the Word and praying. I'm not talking about a 5-10-minute daily devotion. I'm talking about a commitment—real commitment. Your life is no longer your own life. It belongs to Christ. (1 Cor 6:19-20).

That is what we must realize. We're need to live our lives as Christ meant for us to live them. In doing that, we are being *obedient*. As I stated before, we have to be "coachable" in order to be blessed.

Yes, I said coachable. Charles Stanley teaches a good deal on this subject. He teaches that we are to be blindly obedient, no matter what the situation looks like. It's not our job to work everything out or to be all-knowing. It is our job to obey and let God handle the rest. No matter what you see, it is never greater than what God can do. We just need to do what that old hymn tells us—we need to trust and obey.

I tried to think myself into being happy, prosperous, abundant and all the other things I wanted. It wasn't something I could do because I lacked belief. You see, when a thought forms in your mind, it will take you to other thoughts. You can't help that first thought, but you can help where you take it. What I *do* believe is that while we can't think ourselves rich, thin or beautiful, we most certainly can think ourselves into being faithful.

To be faithful is to be committed. We need to be committed to the cause for Christ. The Word directs us to be mindful. We should literally think about the things we are thinking about. If it isn't rooted and grounded in Christ, extinguish it immediately and shift your thoughts.

I hold a Scripture in my heart that I've based my entire life on since I was released from prison. I feel passionate about this passage, especially living in our society today. Matthew 6:33 teaches us to "…seek first His kingdom and His righteousness, and all these things will be added unto you." That is powerful. That is all-inclusive. That leaves no stone unturned. That is where your purpose begins and ends. That is your road map.

Write that Scripture down and read it daily. Dissect it. Study it. Read it and reread it. Live it. Allow it to become part of who you are every single day. When your thoughts tell you that God can't, be assured that He can. He can do *all things*. He is a limitless God. This is His promise to *you*.

Let me correct myself, there is *one* thing God *cannot* do, and that is lie. I encourage you to embrace this Scripture and ask God to reveal these things to you for your own life. I believe that He sent this message just for you, in this moment. He thought enough of you to orchestrate my life and this entire book, just for *you*. I'm not writing to the masses. I am speaking to *you*.

I know you were looking for a magical formula, a process, a secret sauce. I've been exactly where you are at right now. To find your purpose is not impossible. It just takes a shift in perspective and perception. Honestly, you already know what your purpose is. You simply haven't grown to be thankful for it and appreciate it yet.

Perhaps you will think to yourself that it seems so insignificant that it surely can't be your purpose. It just seems so small. But God made you with this purpose. The things that are part of who you already are will be how He equips you because He planned it just for you. This is how you will leave your imprint upon the world. It's your signature. This is your final curtain call. This alone is what is meant for you. How will you be remembered? What legacy will you leave behind if this should be your last day?

You already hold the key. All you need to do is place that key in the door and He will open the door to the future that is waiting for just you. He has plans for you. It is up to you to trust Him enough to take that bold step forward and embrace that purpose. It is good enough. I assure you, the moment you begin to walk in your purpose and use your gifts, He will entrust you with even more. Become faithful in little and He will bless you with much.

Live your life on purpose with passion in Jesus's name.

God bless you.

A Letter from My Pastor

"He who trusts in his own heart is a fool, But he who walks wisely will be delivered." Proverbs 28:26

A friend in ministry suggested that I include a message to any of my readers who may have never known Christ as their Savior. I thought this was a good idea and so I reached out to my pastor and asked him for a letter addressed to you. I pray this letter encourages you to pursue Christ and your purpose with passion.

A Word from Pastor Doug Cooper

Hickory Grove International Pentecostal Holiness Church (HGIPHC)

The Gospel of Jesus Christ is the message that opens the door for anyone to have a right relationship with God. It doesn't matter how far away from God you may have drifted, how many sins you may have committed, or how bad a person you may think you are. The Gospel of Jesus is a message of forgiveness, hope, life, freedom and purpose.

The gospel message starts with bad news. The bad news is that we're all sinners. The preacher and the drug dealer are both in the same boat. Both were born into sin and both need someone to save them from their sin. Romans 3:23 says, "for all have sinned and fall short of the glory of God." This sin causes all to be separated from God and also carries a heavy penalty. Romans 6:23 says, "For the wages of sin is death..." This is not just physical death, but eternal death in the hell.

However, the gospel ends with Good News because God did something that we could not do for ourselves. Romans 5:8 says, "But God demonstrates His own love towards us, in that while we were sinners, Christ died for us."

Let me explain what I mean by that: Prison is used as a punishment for those who commit crimes. In the same manner, God set eternal death in hell as punishment for those who commit sin—which can be considered to be crimes against the Lord. However, to save us from the penalty and punishment for sin, God sent His Son Jesus to earth on our behalf. Jesus willingly died on the cross, taking our place in death. He was our substitute and took the punishment we deserved. Jesus resurrection from the dead on the third day proved that God had accepted His death as the payment for our sins!

Listen! The Good News gets even better! The only response to this Good News that is needed for salvation is to simply believe in the work Jesus Christ did on our behalf! He died for our sins and arose from the grave! Because of what He did through His death and resurrection, he offers salvation—forgiven sin and eternal life as a free gift of his grace. You can't buy it, work for it, or even beg for it. You only need to do what the Bible says:

A LETTER FROM MY PASTOR

- Acknowledge that you're a sinner before a holy God and that your sins have separated you from Him. Romans 3:10 says, "There is none righteous, no, not one." 1 John 1:8 says, "If we say that we have no sin, we deceive ourselves…"

- Ask God to forgive you of your sins. You can do this at church, at home, in your vehicle, or even in a prison cell! The Bible makes this promise in 1 John 1:9: "If we will confess our sins, He is faithful and just to forgive us our sins and to cleanse us from all unrighteousness."

- Believe in your heart and confess with your mouth that Jesus is your Lord and Savior. Romans 10:9-10 says, "that if you confess with your mouth the Lord Jesus and believe in your heart that God has raised Him from the dead, you will be saved. For with the heart one believes unto righteousness, and with the mouth confession is made unto salvation."

- Finally, receive God's grace into your life through simple faith alone! Grace can be explained with this acronym: **G**od's **R**iches **A**t **C**hrist's **E**xpense. Jesus paid for all of your sins, just as the Bible says in Romans 8:1: "There is therefore now no condemnation to those who are in Christ Jesus, who do not walk according to the flesh, but according to the Spirit."

If anyone wants to know Jesus, the following prayer is a tool that I use to help people talk to the Lord to receive the gift of salvation—forgiven sin and eternal life

PRISON TO PROSPERITY WITH PURPOSE

"Dear Jesus. I know that I'm a sinner in need of a Savior. I know that I can't save myself. But today I'm ready to put my trust in You. I'm ready to receive Your grace. I ask that you come into my heart, forgive me of all my sins, and make me right with God. I believe you are the Son of God who died for my sins and rose again on the third day. Today I confess you as my Lord and Savior. In Jesus name I pray. Amen."

I believe that anyone who prays this prayer in faith, with the right motivation is given the wonderful gift of salvation through Jesus Christ. Now's it's time to live out that faith.

Always remember, if you have trusted in Christ Jesus, the Lord God does not condemn you. He loves you. John 3:16 says, "For God so loved the world that He gave His only begotten Son, that whoever believes in Him should not perish but have everlasting life." That life begins today! In Jesus' Name!

There is so much more that could be said concerning this Good News of Jesus. The Bible contains sixty-six books that are filled with this Good News. I encourage you, and all who will read this wonderful book, to also read the Bible, stay connected to a local church and pray often.

I know the Holy Spirit Who is sent to us from God Himself will lead and guide each of us as we follow God's plan and purpose!

Sincerely,
Pastor Doug Cooper

Connecting with Marsha to Speak

I trust that you have been encouraged reading Marsha's story of how God took her from "Prison to Prosperity with Purpose."

She is a trophy of God's grace, and her desire is to help you get from whatever has you imprisoned to a place of freedom, joy, peace and prosperity with purpose in the Lord. Although this doesn't exclude the possibility of material prosperity, that's not all the foundation of the meaning of this book. Rather, it's about living out a life that is abundant in the blessings that only a close personal relationship with Jesus Christ can bring.

Marsha continues to develop her ministry of encouragement to followers across the country through her Facebook page, her website and her podcasts—and she would love to have the opportunity to speak in your church, business, school, event or conference. She also is available to host online events as well. She understands finding and living out your purpose certainly spans all areas of life.

If you would like to inquire about schedules and booking you can contact her through her Prison to Prosperity with Purpose Facebook page, through her webpage at prisontoprosperity.info, or her email address at prisontoprosperity@gmail.com.

Thank you and God bless!

Made in the USA
Coppell, TX
05 November 2023

23843196R10075